Searching for God

Searching for God

Amy Newcombe

iUniverse, Inc.
Bloomington

Searching for God

iUniverse books may be ordered through booksellers or by contacting:

iUniverse
1663 Liberty Drive
Bloomington, IN 47403
www.iuniverse.com
1-800-Authors (1-800-288-4677)

ISBN: 978-1-4620-4583-9 (sc)
ISBN: 978-1-4620-4584-6 (ebk)

Printed in the United States of America

iUniverse rev. date: 09/20/2011

Contents

Chapter 1

A New Home

Tick tock. I could hear the distinct sound of a clock ticking, getting louder and louder with each furious pump of the bike pedals. The sound was actually my heart racing as I rode my purple three-speed over to my father's house. I was in a hurry—and didn't even mind the beads of sweat rolling into my eyes—because I was on my way to find out if my father and his wife Julie were going to let me move in with them.

It took me about ten minutes to get there from my mother's on a normal day, but I think I clocked in at eight minutes on that day.

My father and Julie lived on a corner house in Oxford, New York in the summer of 1979. They lived with Julie's four children from a previous marriage. The oldest, Mary, had graduated from high school a year earlier and went into the military. Wayne was twelve; he was the only boy, and he blasted "My Sharona" and "Hot Stuff" from the boom box in his room pretty much every day. The youngest were identical twin girls named Cindy and Susan. I thought it was the greatest thing in the world to have a set of twins. I wished I would have twins someday.

1

I knew at fourteen I wanted more out of life, and that's why I was pedaling my way to my father's. I felt he could provide me with more of a "normal" family life than my mother, which would allow me to be a better version of myself. I thought I would enjoy having a brother and two sisters, and I wanted to have a closer relationship with my dad.

At my mother's, life was pretty lonely; she worked nights, and I was at school during the day. I hoped moving in with my father would relieve my mother of the financial burden of providing food, clothes, and shelter for me as well—my father had more money. I didn't consider my mother's feelings when I asked if I could live with my father's family. I was very self-centered as a young teenager; life was all about me.

I parked my bike on the patio in the back of my father's house, since we used the back door to come in and out. I didn't have to knock. I walked right in and said, "Good morning, how is everybody?"

"Why are you out of breath?" Cindy asked. She had a towel wrapped around her head and another around her torso as she grabbed a carton of milk from the fridge.

"I rode my bike as fast as I could, and I'm just catching my breath," I answered with a shrug, throwing my hands on my hips.

"Hi Emily Jane! Come on in here," Julie shouted from the living room.

I loved it when Julie would call me by my first and middle name. For the most part, she only called me "Emily" if I was in trouble. That's how I would know something was wrong.

My heart was still pounding, but I couldn't hear the clock anymore. I patted my chest to try to get it to slow down.

I walked through the kitchen and into the dining room, where Julie and my father were sitting at the table under a delicate chandelier.

"Your father and I have decided you can move in this June," Julie said as soon as I walked in the room.

"Wow! Thank you! That's great!" I replied, shocked and overwhelmed with excitement. This was the beginning of something great, I thought. This could lead to a new and improved me.

We discussed rules and expectations, which weren't as extensive as I thought they would be. I was to get up and go to school, come home from school, do homework, eat dinner, help with chores when asked, and on the weekends I was to come in when the streetlights turned on.

My mother had similar rules, but I often took advantage of them because the consequences were not consistent.

I had a boyfriend named Daniel at the time. He was tall, with blond hair and blue eyes. We rode bikes together to the park and to the outdoor swimming pool, and I was allowed to see him out in public but not be alone with him at my house or his.

My father had a hard time being sensitive with his choice of words whenever I mentioned my boyfriend.

Chapter 2

A Breakdown

For two weeks in August every year, my dad and Julie would go on a vacation. That particular summer, I would stay with my mother while Julie's kids went out west to visit their father. My mother lived about a mile away; I could visit her any time my father and Julie were home, but I didn't.

Mom lived in a nice three-bedroom apartment close by. We would usually come in and out the back door, just like at my father's house. It was a two-family home, with an apartment upstairs. It was always kind of dark in the apartment, thanks to the tall oak trees surrounding the house. On hot and muggy days, the apartment stayed very cool.

My sister Connie had the bigger bedroom. I didn't care; Mom said it would be easier for me to keep my room clean—that was the room's selling point—but I never bothered with that. It was usually a huge mess of clothes, books, teen magazines, and just general garbage. On Saturdays, we turned off the TV at 12:00 PM and cleaned our bedrooms and did chores around the house. But if our bedrooms were messy by Tuesday or Wednesday, Mom didn't fuss.

My room at my father's, on the other hand, was *always* expected to be neat and tidy.

The living room at Mom's had a shaggy brownish rug, which she had moved with us for about four years. Candy, our English springer spaniel, could often be found curled up on that rug. She'd be sweet and content until someone walked in the room, and then her tail would wag and shake her small body from side to side.

We had simple furniture: a couch and a chair. Our television was a very small nine-inch color set, but we didn't notice how small it was, because we were so used to it. I watched *The Brady Bunch*, *Little House on the Prairie*, *Happy Days*, and *Laverne and Shirley* on that set every week until it was my bedtime.

My mother's bedroom was off the eat-in kitchen; I think it was meant to be a dining room, but Mom made it into her bedroom. The bathroom was off the kitchen, and I had to duck while taking a shower because the showerhead was so low. I was tall for my age: five foot eight at fourteen years old.

I was not picked on about my height, thank God. But because I was taller and looked older, people expected me to act more mature. I did just the opposite—I was immature and very dependent.

During my first visit with my mom since moving out of her house, she came into the living room late one night. We had our most intense conversation of the summer and of my life; I believe it changed me forever.

Mom was talking about Grandma and Dad. She talked on and on about how much money Grandma spent on the four of us when my sister and I were babies. She would spend money on our food, clothing, shelter, medical bills, etc. The conversation started to get uncomfortable when my mother decided to tell me something very personal.

"Emily, I need to tell you something," she began. "I don't think your father ever loved me; he married me because I was pregnant with you. Abortions were illegal then, and he thought the right thing to do was to get married." She had tears in her eyes.

I sat next to my mother on the couch, wide-eyed and shifting my weight from one hip to the other and back again.

"So what happened after you got married?" I asked.

"Your father talked me into leaving New York and moving to Iowa to stay with his aunt and uncle on a farm. Your great-aunt and great-uncle were wonderful and loving people who took me and your father in until you were born."

"When did you come to New York?"

"You were four months old, and we came back to Hamilton just in time for your father to return to college," Mom said.

"Were you happy?"

"I was happy at first. I had a terrible childhood growing up with Granny. I originally wanted to go to a home for unwed mothers, and I didn't know what the plan was after that. But getting married was just a better alternative," Mom said.

I didn't ask my mom any more questions; instead, I assured her that Daniel and I were not going to have sex. I got the sense she was telling me this story as a sort of warning against my relationship with Daniel. I told her we were just really good friends and enjoyed each other's company.

The last few days of my first visit with my mother were on the quiet side. I was still overwhelmed with the information she had shared. It bothered me a lot when I thought about it; I was very confused about my place in the family. And just who was my father, really?

I returned to my father's house and started eighth grade on the following Tuesday. It was my last year before high school, and I was taking all the usual courses plus seventh grade science. I was a little overwhelmed taking both grades of science at once.

Daniel and I were in the same social studies class. There weren't enough textbooks to go around in the class, so Daniel and I volunteered to share a book. My father was not very happy when he found out. I'm pretty sure he was under the impression Daniel and I were going to have sex or at least do more flirting than homework.

The year prior, I received a 100 percent on a sex education test. It was easy for me because it was basically a test on the different parts of the body.

Instead of a pat on the back or a "congratulations," my father asked, "Did you get the 100 percent because of your knowledge or your experience?"

I didn't answer; instead, I stared at my feet. Later, I told my mother what he said. She told me I should have answered him by saying, "It was because of *your* experience, Dad." She said she grew suspicious of my father when he was in college. Apparently, he was spending far too much time "at the library" for her liking. She didn't elaborate much, and I didn't pester her for more information.

I had English, which I didn't mind at all, because I loved to write. I was taking physics and chemistry, which were pretty boring; it was all I could do to stay awake. I was also taking math and didn't have too much trouble as long as I kept up with the homework.

I was also in choir, concert band, and marching band. We had choir rehearsal twice a week and concert or marching band three times a week. I played the clarinet for a little more than three years—and played very well, I might add.

Choir was a lot of fun, and we had a Christmas concert every year. One of my favorite parts of choir was the warm-ups. Some of the tunes were very silly; sometimes the warm-ups got us laughing when we messed up, and we'd have to start all over again. I wanted to be a soprano with a beautiful, feminine voice, but I sang with the altos that year.

Gym was a challenge for me. I was not very athletic; I was tall and didn't run very fast. But I tried hard, participated in class, and got good grades.

I was also required to take Home Economics, studying early childhood development. For one particular class project, the students were asked to find some photographs taken when we were babies. We were supposed to put together a collage of these photos and stick it in a cube.

I could sense almost instantly that this was not going to be a successful project for me. It was emotionally stressful. My father was in college when my sister and I were babies, and my parents were married when all the baby pictures were taken.

I knew Dad had about 250 slides of photos taken when we were babies; we had just looked at them over the summer when Grandma came up to visit for the Fourth of July. Baby pictures of my sister and me were a reminder of the past and not Julie's favorite subject (she was very focused on building a future with my father, not dwelling on the past). Grandma and I were not thoughtful and would bring up old stories about the past often.

This project was not going to go over well, even if I could get up enough courage to ask about the baby pictures. I remember thinking of myself as the Cowardly Lion in *The Wizard of Oz.* I was humming "If I Only Had a Brain . . . a heart . . . the nerve" to myself.

I started to become very nervous and agitated about completing this assignment. I couldn't ask my father about the baby pictures; it was just not possible. I also wouldn't think to ask my mother for any baby pictures. Dad had the majority of them, and Mom wouldn't part with the few she had. I didn't know how I was going to do this project.

I started to feel overwhelmed with sadness and began obsessing about how my father never loved my mother. I didn't know how to forget what my mother told me, as much as I wanted to. I also wondered what my life would be like if my parents never got married. Maybe my mom would have gone to that home for unwed mothers, or maybe I would have been adopted.

There was a lot of stuff going on at once. My knee had been swollen at the time, and I was in a lot of pain. My big bone was rubbing on the smaller bone. This stupid project for Home Economics was making me an emotional wreck. It was also a bad idea to share my social studies book with my boyfriend. He was tall and cute, but he had issues.

Daniel lived with his father; he never said where his mother was. He had two younger sisters and one younger brother, and they lived in a nice house with nice stuff. I liked Daniel. He was taller than me (not many people were at that age), had blond hair, and blue eyes.

He had a pale complexion that turned a shade or two darker in the summer. He was on the thin side and dressed nice.

My father was not in favor of this relationship. I know if he had just talked to me about what he was thinking; it would have been easier for all of us. He probably thought that Daniel, fifteen years old and one year my senior, would eventually con me into sex. But the truth is we weren't even thinking about sex; he only kissed me on the cheek.

I was very stressed over this Home Economics project; it was making me really nuts. I was sure I was going to fail this class because I couldn't ask my dad about my baby photos. I couldn't understand it; I didn't know why I had to do this stupid project. Julie was strict and I had a respectful fear of her.

I was so upset and so overwhelmed, and I was beginning to feel confused.

I went to see the guidance counselor after class one day, and I told him about the conversation I had with my mother about my parent's relationship.

I was getting more and more confused. I liked Daniel, but I didn't love him. It was fun to hang out with him, but I really didn't want any more than that. I was not thinking too clearly, and life seemed to be going in slow motion. I didn't know what was happening to me. I felt sad, lost, and confused.

I was so worried about my parents. They were divorced and got back together once when I was younger. I'd always counted on them getting back together again, for good. I was going deeper into my own world and my own head. I stopped practicing my clarinet. I was not talking to any of my friends. I hated science; it was a lot of work to double up, and I was getting behind in writing assignments in English. I was even having a hard time in gym class.

On September 14, I was standing in the parking lot at the back of the junior high school. I had all of my textbooks and my clarinet with me. I was looking down at the ground, and I was unable to see straight. I wasn't quite sure where I was, who I was, or what to do with myself.

Julie pulled up in Old Bessie, her light brown station wagon with wood paneling down the middle. She saw me standing perfectly still (my psychologist, years later, used the word "catatonic"). I saw Julie lean over, and she rolled down the passenger side window.

"Get in the car, Emily Jane," she said.

I can't remember the ride to the pediatrician's office. I can't remember talking to the doctor. I do recall overhearing the adults talking about "path one, path two, and path three."

I cracked up. I had totally lost my mind. I had to take Stelazine, a strong medication that made my mouth dry, and I took Cogentin with it. It was supposed to help me snap back to my old self. I couldn't go to school. My father said, "You aren't well. When you are well, you can go to school."

It was official, I was sick in the head. I had an appointment with a psychiatrist. (The theme song from "Close Encounters of the Third Kind" seems fitting.)

At first, I saw an adolescent psychiatrist with a very thick Indian accent. I had a hard time understanding him when he asked me questions. But my mother demanded I see a child psychiatrist instead; she apparently didn't think I was a very mature fourteen-year-old. I changed within a week's time to see a child psychiatrist, Dr. Brown.

During my recovery, I was home with Julie while the kids were at school. My stepmom quit her job to stay home with me. On a school day, I got up at about 10:00 AM. I would go downstairs for breakfast, and the kids would leave out a couple cereal boxes for me to choose from. They would also leave out a bowl, a spoon, and a napkin.

I spent most of the day watching morning shows, including *The Price Is Right*. I watched channel three soap operas faithfully, Monday through Friday. I had this same routine for about three weeks.

I had this beautiful, furry, baby blue robe I would wear all day over pajamas. The medication made my mouth dry and my lips were very chapped—so chapped they looked raw and sometimes bled. My father gave me orange-flavored ChapStick.

In the family room of my father's house there was an antique mirror. My father had me go up to the mirror, take out my ChapStick, and apply it to my lips. He showed me how to do this several times.

The guidance counselor at school had called up my father and Julie to discuss our previous meeting, where I had rehashed the conversation I had with my mother. Dad and Julie came to the conclusion that my nervous breakdown was a direct result of the conversation with my mother. I was unable to see her for a while, but after a few weeks, I was able to speak with her on the phone.

Around this time, my father took it upon himself to end my relationship with Daniel. Daniel had not seen me in school for four or five days. I lived about a block and a half away from the school, so he came over to see why I had been absent. My father told him I had mono, "the kissing disease." He wouldn't give Daniel any more information, and Daniel and I lost touch. I had no idea this happened until years later. Shortly after I was out of school, Daniel and his sisters were taken away from their father and placed into foster care.

When my mother and Daniel were taken away from me, I knew my world would never be the same.

Chapter 3

Innocence Lost

It was a Monday, shortly after I was taken out of school, and Julie was bringing me to therapy. It was a dark and dreary fall day; it was foggy out but not raining.

Dr. Brown came out to the waiting room and called my name. He was handsome for a psychiatrist; he was about an inch taller than me with a medium build. His skin was fairly tan, and he had dark brown hair that was starting to thin on top. I went back with him, and Julie stayed in the waiting room.

The office we went into was cramped and ugly. The doctor's desk was pretty impressive and had a full leather chair for him to sit in, but there was only a folding chair for me. The walls were painted an unattractive off-yellow color, and there was one dirty window in the room with no curtain. A very thick, worn-out brown carpet covered the floor.

The meeting only lasted fifty minutes. Dr. Brown asked me a bunch of questions, starting with, "Do you hear voices?"

I told him I did not, and after talking for another twenty to twenty-five minutes, he asked me again, "Do you hear voices?" Again, I said, "No."

His voice was so soft I could barely hear him. He didn't offer conversation. He responded often with, "What do you think?" and "How does that make you feel?" And every chance he got, he snuck in, "Do you hear voices?"

After he asked me about voices for the third or fourth time, I recalled a conversation I overheard Dad and Julie having while they were pissed off at each other. I told Dr. Brown about the conversation because I could recall it from memory, therefore "hearing" their "voices" in my head. He didn't understand that it was a memory I was recalling, but he did stop asking that question over and over.

I was relieved when the session was finished. I went out to the front room, and Julie was waiting for me. When we got in the car, "The Sounds of Silence" by Simon and Garfunkel played.

I was seeing Dr. Brown every Monday. During one particular session, I decided to open up about events in my childhood. I told him about the time my babysitter's brother touched me. I was about four years old.

"We lived on a hill, in a white house in Oxford," I began. "We had a fenced-in backyard, with a sandbox and swing set. I loved to be in my backyard on the swings. Our neighbor had a teenage daughter, Terry. She babysat now and then when my parents went out. She had a younger brother named Michael, and he liked to walk by our backyard every day to talk. We trusted Terry, so we trusted Michael too.

"One day, Michael walked over to our house and started to talk to my sister and me. We were in the backyard. I was four and my sister Connie was three and a half." I could picture my sister as she looked that day, in her red-and-white plaid pants and orange shirt with matching plaid tie. I was wearing the same outfit.

"Even though I was only four going on five, I looked like I was six or seven years old," I continued. "I was taller than Connie, looked older, and I was much friendlier and talkative. I remember I was on the swing that day when Michael walked by and said, 'Hey girls, wanna play at the playground?'

"I said, 'Sure, when do you want to go?' He said, 'How about right now?' I was swinging on the swing in my backyard. I started going higher and higher and counted, 'One, two, and three!' Then I jumped off the swing and couldn't wait to go to the playground with my sister and Michael.

"He was eleven or twelve years old, I think. He looked like a teenager because he was big for his age. He was Italian and had olive skin, a husky build, and long, straight black hair. He always wore black t-shirts and blue jeans. That day he had a black sweatshirt with a hood. I think black was his favorite color. And I don't think he changed his clothes much, because he always smelled musty.

"Connie, Michael, and I were the only ones at the playground. First, we got on the swings—I loved the swings. Michael was pushing me and then Connie, but he got bored after a while and wanted to kick a ball around that he found.

"I said, 'Okay.' I jumped off the swing, helped my sister, and then we started tossing the ball back and forth. After tossing it around a few times, he kicked the ball way, way out into the field near the woods.

"We all chased the ball and started kicking it. The final kick was from Michael, and he kicked it far into the woods. It was chilly outside and the woods were not a very nice place. It was colder and darker there because the trees blocked the sun.

"Michael told me to wait when we first walked into the woods. He took Connie by her hand and walked into the woods until I couldn't see them anymore. I told him as he walked away, 'Don't take too long.'

"While I was standing in the dark and scary woods, I heard a loud noise. It was a squirrel rustling up some leaves. This scared me, and I jumped. Then some birds flew over my head, making more noise. I got very anxious, and I decided to scream '*Michael!*' Michael and Connie came back to where I was standing pretty fast.

"Michael sounded out of breath and asked, 'What's the matter?' I told him I was scared, and he called me a 'big baby.' I said, 'You need to take us home right now!' And he treated me like a baby and called me names all the way back to the house.

Dr. Brown then asked me the official shrink question, "How did that make you feel?"

"I don't remember; it was nine years ago," I said.

"Oh, time is up. We have to end."

"Okay, but there's more. I'll tell you next time."

"Okay Emily, you can do that," Dr. Brown said.

When I got in the car with Julie, another popular song was playing on the radio: "Time in a Bottle" by Jim Croce.

Another week went by. I was still getting up late and watching game shows and soap operas in the afternoon. But on Mondays, I was talking to Dr. Brown. I actually looked forward to seeing him because I knew ahead of time what I was going to tell him. I started to feel a little better.

On a Monday in October, Julie and I got into the car to go to my appointment. I was feeling pretty good and couldn't wait to tell Dr. Brown more about Michael.

It was a cloudy day, but the sun was peeking through the clouds on and off. It was warmer than it had been at the start of the school year. Julie was in a good mood, too.

I sat down in the waiting room and Julie signed me in with the receptionist. About five minutes later, Dr. Brown came out to tell me he was ready.

When I sat down in the folding chair in the doctor's dingy office, he asked, "So Emily, how are you today?"

"I'm fine, how are you?" I asked, smiling.

"I'm well, thank you."

Dr. Brown started to talk, but I interrupted him and said, "Oh yeah, you'll be surprised to hear what happened the second time. My sister was taking a nap in the house, and I trusted Michael because nothing happened to me the first time. I was in my backyard again, swinging, and here came Michael again. I should call him Mr. Greaseball.

"He said, 'Wanna play on the playground again?' He had a look on his face that should have been suspicious to me, but I didn't feel afraid," I paused for a moment and let out a big sigh. "I loved to swing, so of course I went. So . . . well . . ."

"What's wrong Emily?" Dr. Brown asked.

"Please, this is not easy for me. Don't rush me. So off I went to the playground, alone with Michael this time. He pushed me on the swing for about ten minutes. I jumped off very high in the air for a five-year-old. Oh yeah, I had a birthday after the first time, so I was five now. It was warmer this time, and I had a short dress on. I might have had shorts on underneath, but I can't remember.

"I remember the sky was very blue and there were no clouds and no breeze. My hair was up in pigtails, and I had on a plaid purple dress and my white tennis sneakers.

"Michael led me into the woods when I was done swinging. I can't remember how he sweet-talked me into following him. I think I went because I didn't have any fear that he was going to leave me or anything. We walked around for about five minutes, then Michael noticed a clearing and we sat down. He started to sweet-talk me. He said I was pretty and smart.

"I don't know how he knew I was smart, because I hadn't started school yet. But I believed him. Then he somehow talked me into pulling down my pants and lying down," I said, my voice growing softer. "He took his fingers and touched my privates. I don't remember him hurting me. It wasn't long after he was touching me that we heard some people talking. Michael's friends were in the area and walking real close to where we had stopped. He stopped what he was doing kind of fast, and I pulled up my pants. Then we walked out of the woods. I didn't know we did anything wrong, but I also didn't tell anyone what happened."

"So, what do you know now?" Dr. Brown asked.

"I know he shouldn't have touched me," I replied. My back was starting to hurt from the uncomfortable folding chair.

"Oh Emily, I'm sorry. Our time is up. We will continue next week, okay?"

"Yup, see you next time," I said happily, adding, "I guess I am really relieved I don't have that secret anymore."

"I'm glad it's not a secret anymore, too," he said, with a sad smile on his face.

We said goodbye, and I went with Julie to the car. She mentioned I would be going back to school the following week. I was happy about that; it had been three long weeks, and I thought I was ready. "Coming Around Again" by Carly Simon came on the radio.

Chapter 4

New Family Dynamics

It had been three weeks since my nervous breakdown, and Dr. Brown suggested my father send me back to school.

It was a Monday morning in October, and the outside air was crisp. I had laid out all my clothes for school the night before. I had a silky, baby blue, semi-sheer blouse I was going to wear, and it had a matching scarf to go with it. I was also going to wear khaki-colored corduroys and shoes handed down to me from my dad. I had rather large feet for a girl my age.

It was about 7:20 AM, and I was standing in my room, looking at all my schoolbooks. I went downstairs in a hurry and suddenly couldn't remember why I was there. I went back up to my room and continued to stare at all my schoolbooks. I wondered how was I going to get organized enough to return to school. I went downstairs again, and because I seemed disjointed and confused, my father immediately said, "Nope, you're not going back to school. What's the guidance counselor's name again?"

"It's Mr. Harris, Dad," I softly and slowly replied.

"Okay, go back upstairs. Take your school clothes off and relax, right now."

"Yes, Dad."

Mr. Harris came over within the hour and met with Dad and Julie. My parents and the guidance counselor agreed to an in-home tutor for me Monday through Thursday afternoons. During this time, Julie would run errands and do whatever she needed to do.

I also had an appointment with Dr. Brown that afternoon. I thought highly of the doctor's opinions, and when I went in, he did not seem surprised or disappointed that I couldn't go to school.

"How are you feeling today?" Dr. Brown asked.

"I'm okay, but . . . I wish I could see my mother."

"Why don't you tell me about your mother?"

That put a big, cheesy smile on my face. "Okay, let me describe my mom to you," I replied. "Mom's name is Karen, and she has one brother, Nicholas. My mother's parents met in the military; my Granny is from one of the European countries. Unfortunately, she was a heavy drinker and still is. She drinks vodka straight, usually, with a few ice cubes. She's horrible when she's drinking; she can say some really awful things.

"She doesn't really like my mother, because Mom had my sister and me at a young age. She also didn't like my father. But Mom has a decent relationship with my grandfather. He works evenings and leaves my Granny home alone, bored and with no car—she stopped driving at a young age."

"Emily, so far you've told me about your mother's parents, but what about your mother?" Dr. Brown asked.

"Okay, okay, I'm getting to her. Well, my mother is five feet tall. My father, who you've seen, is a giant; that's why I'm so tall. Mom has big, deep blue eyes and a pale complexion. She has naturally curly brown hair, and she's not fat or skinny; she's just in the middle somewhere."

"Okay, Emily, that's what she looks like. What else?"

"Well, Mom didn't learn about sex from her mother, like how she told me about it. She was sent to an Episcopal church to learn about it, but I don't think she went," I said with a laugh. "Mom works the night shift at the hospital as a nurse's aide. She works all the time, I don't know, maybe because my Dad doesn't pay much in child support. But she works at night, I think, because it pays more than during the day. During the day, while my sister and I went to school, she stayed home and would sleep. Then she would get up, make dinner, and be home when we would go to bed. While my sister and I slept, Mom would be at work.

"We also spent many vacations and summers with our grandparents. They lived just outside of Hamilton. We were safe and entertained—well, except that Granny C. drank like a fish sometimes, but then we kept ourselves out of her hair and stayed in the bedroom.

"I spent more time with Grandma Washborne. I was her first granddaughter. I enjoyed going to her house because I had one on one attention.

"My sister spent most of her time with Mom's parents. When we went to their house in the suburbs, we had friends in the neighborhood, and we were more independent. Grandma on Dad's side liked to control everything we did, and she lived in the city.

"Grandma Washborne was frustrated at times when my parents first got married. She paid for everything for the first six years of my life and again when we moved back to Hamilton. My parents lived in student housing while Dad was in college, and Grandma's money was really my parent's only source of income. When I got older, even when we moved to Oxford and Dad got a job, Grandma still paid for some things.

"She liked to rub it in my face if she spent money on me, but she did that with everybody. When I was six years old, she showed me check stubs and payments she made for my parents when I was a baby. Mom told me that when she tried to get a job at a downtown department store, Grandma was not supportive in any way. Grandma told her that by the time Mom paid for carfare, childcare, and bought lunch, she would not be making any money. So why work? But I think Mom just wanted a few dollars for herself.

"I was about a year old when my mom realized she was pregnant again. This really didn't sit too well with Grandma. Grandma thought one child was plenty while Dad was still in college and trying to make it. She was really stretched financially, spending a lot of money on just the three of us.

"And Grandma has always been very controlling. Mom told me she had a big fight with Grandma while she was pregnant with my sister. Do you want me to tell you about it?" I asked the doctor.

"Sure, go ahead," he replied.

"I was really small, and my mother was about four months pregnant with my sister. We were visiting Grandma at her house, and I was upstairs taking a nap. Grandma approached my mother and said she wanted to talk to her.

"Then she asked my mother, 'Would you consider signing papers to have Emily stay with me, in the event anything happens to you before, during, or after you give birth to this next baby?' Mom said this question made her very angry.

"Mom said, 'I am twenty years old, having a second baby, and I am in great health. You are asking too much!' Mom said they started yelling at each other. This was one time my mother didn't give in. She wasn't wishy-washy about her answer; she was crystal clear."

"Emily, how does that make you feel?" Dr. Brown asked.

"Pretty good, actually," I responded. "I don't think it would have been a good thing for me to live with my grandmother. Anyway, I had a wonderful childhood when my sister and I were babies. Then when my Dad was hired by the hospital, we moved to Oxford."

Dr. Brown asked, "What happened after moving to Oxford?"

"We moved to a house on a hill, and that's when Michael touched me. I already told you about that. We moved again to the big house on the main street, and that's when I started elementary school.

"I was a good student. I didn't get into too much trouble, because I knew there were consequences with Mom and Dad. Kindergarten was good; except my mother told me she wanted the school to have me repeat kindergarten. They refused.

"I remember first grade to be okay. I learned basic reading and math; I also remember being rambunctious and getting into trouble. I think I used to giggle and say the word "fart" repeatedly when the teacher was out of the room. For the most part, I did well in first grade.

"At the end of first grade, my father was transferred to the Midwest. We moved before July 4; I remember going to see the fireworks out there. It was awesome! We had sparklers that I got to hold and watch them go out, even when I was seven years old. I think—"

Dr. Brown interrupted, "Emily, time is up. You can tell me about the Midwest in our next session."

After the session was over, I went out to the waiting room and Julie was waiting patiently for me. When we got in the car, Jim Croce's "Bad, Bad Leroy Brown" played on the radio. I thought it was a crazy song because it had the word "damn" in it, and we weren't allowed to say that word.

It seemed as though I blinked and the next thing I knew it was Monday. It was time for therapy again.

"Okay, so where did I leave off?" I began, pausing for a moment. "Oh yeah, we moved to the Midwest because my dad was transferred to another hospital. We lived in this really big white house on the corner of a street. That was when everything fell apart for my parents.

"Grandma Washborne and my mother told me at separate times that my parent's relationship was in trouble anyway. This was just a way for things to end faster."

"Okay, so what happened?" Dr. Brown asked.

"Dad met the woman across the street and liked her, and Mom found out. Mom packed up while we were taking a nap one afternoon and drove back to Morrisville. We stayed at our grandparents. Dad drove back to New York to talk to Mom; they decided Connie would go back to live with Dad and his new family, and I would stay with my mom."

"Okay, are you talking about Julie?" Dr. Brown asked.

"Yes, I am. It was actually fun because we used to go over to Julie's house and play with Mary and Wayne before my parents split up.

"Mary is Julie's oldest daughter. She just turned eleven at the time, and her younger brother Wayne was three. The youngest were identical twin girls. They were sixteen months old when we met them.

"During the summer, we did some creative projects with Mary. She created a home movie theatre in a box. First, she would take a box and put it on its side, cutting the four flaps off. Then she would put two holes in the box, one on each side. Next, she would find two sticks about twelve inches long. She would write out a story, include drawings, tape the paper together, and tape it around one stick. Then she would curl the paper around the stick on one side and tape the last piece of paper to the other stick on the other side.

"Then, as you looked directly at the box, you could take your hands and move the stick around, and the paper with the story on it would go across the little stage area of the box. Once, we drew *The Wizard of Oz* on paper. We made some curtains out of scrap material for the box to make it look like a theatre. We spent the night a few times in Julie's basement with Mary. That was a lot of fun, too.

"One night when we slept over, we stayed up to watch a monster movie. The basement was a big room. It had light brown wall paneling for walls, and the floor had a thin carpet—I think it was a dark green. The room had a foldout bed and a small TV. We jumped on the beds and would yell, 'Fart, fart, fart!'

"My sister and I were used to scary monster movies because we watched them with my Dad. We watched this one monster movie over at Mary's. There was a woman who looked like she lived in the 1950s because of the way she was dressed. She had an apron on over her dress, and she was standing at the kitchen sink, washing her dishes. It was pouring rain in the movie, lightening and thundering. The woman had a see-through curtain at the sink, and she pulled the curtain back because she thought she saw something. All of a sudden, we heard this blood-curdling scream, and there was a man standing outside her window. His clothes were raggedy and soaked, and his face was covered in blood. Me, Connie, and Mary all looked at each other, and then looked at the bottom of the stairs in the basement, where there was a small window with a curtain. We were all really scared for a minute, and then we giggled about it a second later.

"After Dad took Connie back to the Midwest and left me with Mom, Mom and I lived with a woman and her three daughters. I went to a different school for the first part of second grade, just the first six weeks. Then Mom and I moved to an apartment, and I changed schools. Mom's heart ached for my sister Connie for the couple months she was gone.

"I was home after school without supervision around this time. This lack of supervision at seven years old got me into some trouble; I craved the wrong kind of attention. I don't think Mom had the money for a babysitter, and she had to work the day shift at the hospital at this time. I was home after school by myself for about two hours. This wouldn't have been a problem if it weren't for Michael and his buddy Mark catching up with me. Yes, the same Michael who was the babysitter's brother, the one who brought me into the woods. After school one day—"

Dr. Brown interrupted, "I'm sorry, Emily. Time is up, but I'll see you next week."

"Okay, but don't forget where I left off," I said.

"I won't. Have a good week, and I'll see you next time."

"Yup, see you next time," I replied, standing up from my chair.

When Julie and I hopped into the car, Simon and Garfunkel's "Bridge Over Troubled Water" played.

I arrived at the clinic to see Dr. Brown the following Monday. He called me back to his office, and I jumped right back into my story.

"I guess you can tell I like attention," I began. "I invited Mark and Michael to come over to the apartment because my mom wasn't home. It was late October; I remember the weather not being too cold yet. The boys came in and immediately wanted to go into my bedroom, and I let them.

"The boys talked me into lying down on the bed. I kept my clothes on, and they did too. They took turns getting on top of me and humping me. There was no kissing, and we all kept our clothes on. We did this for maybe half an hour, and then my mother came home. She heard voices in the other room; they tried to hide, but she caught them. She cussed them out, and they went running out the door. Afterward, my mother didn't bother to have a talk with me about having the boys in the apartment.

"My father and sister had been in the Midwest since September, and it was getting close to Christmas. My mother missed Connie like crazy, so Dad brought her to our apartment, and she moved back in with us.

"It's funny how I can remember details of conversations, people, and places. But the time from second grade to fourth grade is fuzzy. In that time, I can barely remember what happened, so please don't quote me. I know my parents tried to get back together again. But in one of those Septembers, they broke it off for good. My father then went to the Midwest to get Julie and her four children. He brought them to Oxford. He divorced my mother and married Julie. Then my mother went to nursing school to become a Licensed Practical Nurse. She started seeing a man named Tom.

"In third grade, our class was reading the book *Charlotte's Web*, about the pig named Wilbur. The kids were cruel that year and very critical of my bad habits; I didn't have good table manners. I guess my parents assumed that I knew to chew my food with my mouth closed. I should have known not to talk with my mouth open.

"Well," I continued with a sigh, "my last name starts with a W, so when we were reading about Wilbur, my classmates named me Wilbur Washborne. Then, as I got older, I was tall, had big feet for my age, and wore glasses, so the nickname was extended to Wilbur-Wacky-Big-Foot-Four-Eyes Washborne. This hurt my feelings most of the time. The best the adults could do was to tell me to ignore them. They told me to say, 'Sticks and stones will break my bones, but names will never hurt me.' That's a bunch of bologna. The kids should have been throwing rocks at me instead of calling me names.

"A really fond memory of third and fourth grade was a play I was in. I'm pretty sure it was third grade. I was a very outspoken third grader; I talked a lot, laughed really loud, and just wanted to have fun. We did the play *Pinocchio and the Fire-eater*. Guess what, Dr. Brown?"

"I don't know; what, Emily?" Dr. Brown asked.

"I was the fire-eater because of my loud voice. That was a lot of fun. During the end of third grade, my mom was dating Tom. He is Polish and tall, with blond hair and blue eyes. Every now and then, Tom would try to grow a mustache or a beard, but it wouldn't grow in right, then he'd get mad and shave it off. Anyway, he liked my mother a lot and made her laugh. In the spring of fourth grade, Tom applied for a job at the hospital in Waterville. When he was offered the position, he asked my mother to marry him. They were married in the summer of 1975.

"We moved to a house across the street from the hospital for the first year Mom and Tom were married. It was great to start all over and everything, but I wasn't used to working so hard in school. The standards in Waterville were higher than Oxford. In fact, the passing standard in Oxford was sixty-five, and in Waterville it was seventy-five. I started out in fifth grade at first.

"After two weeks, the school officials had a meeting with my mother and wanted to put me back a grade, in a special education class. I was repeating fourth grade, but in special education. The class was small and the teacher was very nice. One of my neighbors was in my class; we had the same last name, and he was a boy.

"In this class, I was given a different math course than everyone else because my math level was higher. I was good at thinking things through when I took my time. However, I think the other subjects—English, social studies, and science—were at the third grade level.

"Mom and Tom tried to have a life together for about a year. At the end of that year, they decided to split up; I don't know any details. This was okay with me because I was pretty set on my parents getting back together again for the third and last time. Mom, my sister, and I moved to an apartment complex in Waterville.

"Tom moved across the street from the complex; he wasn't over my mother and still had hope. This did not make my mother happy, but, every other weekend; we would go over to Tom's for doughnuts and juice. There was nothing on television, so sometimes we went bowling.

"The summer went by fast, and I went into fifth grade. I stayed in special education and this time went into the fifth and sixth grade combination class. I also had my first male teacher, Mr. Warren. He was almost the same age as Mom, and he was single. Every once in a while we would run into him at the grocery store, and I would tease Mom, saying they should date.

"Fifth grade was a little intense because there were only three girls in my class, plus fifteen boys and me. We were stuck being taught sex education by Mr. Warren, and we weren't separated from the boys. That was not fun. The teacher showed slides of internal sex organs of the girls and boys," I said, bursting out with a laugh. "And he said, 'If you girls want to make any comments, please feel free.' That was goofy. Fifth grade was okay. I got through fine, and then we moved again over the summer. During that summer, something else happened with Michael."

"Okay, Emily. Sorry, time is up," Dr. Brown said.

I went out to the waiting room and there, as always, was Julie. We went out to the car, and I anxiously awaited the song that would play. That day it was "The Chain" by Fleetwood Mac.

Chapter 5

Behind the Pool

The following Monday, I went back to Dr. Brown's office and sat down. "Okay, where did I leave off?"

The doctor responded, "You said you finished fifth grade, and it was 'okay.' And you had another encounter with Michael."

"Okay, I remember now. My sister and I had bikes that we rode to the outdoor pool in Oxford, where my father lived. We were allowed to ride our bikes all over the place. We had combination locks and could lock our bikes up if we stopped at someone's house or the store so they wouldn't get stolen.

"It was a sunny day in the summer, and I was twelve years old. I knew about sex, body parts, and could explain conception of a baby, but I really didn't think about it much. I also had enough common sense to keep my clothes on around boys. Seriously, I didn't realize or actually sit and think about the body parts and what they did until I was older.

"Well anyway, this one particular day in the summer, I rode my bike to the pool and ran into the one and only Michael. I still looked three or four years older than I was because I was tall. Michael said to me, 'Hey Emily, whatcha doing?' I told him I was there to swim, and he asked me to come over to him.

"I don't know why I bothered to acknowledge that Michael was even alive. But here we go again," I said with a sigh. "Michael asked me to go with him behind the pool. I was a little hesitant at first, and he said, 'It's no big deal. Come on.'

"So, not having a care in the world, I ignored my past experience with this guy. I went with the greasy, smelly creep behind the pool. I guess it was because I loved the attention, especially from an older boy. He looked about sixteen. I don't know how old he really was.

"He was a little taller than me and had the same black hair as before, with bangs in his face, but now he also had a very faint mustache and pimples all over. He was still wearing black, but he was wearing shorts instead of jeans. Anyway, he was the same old Michael, with the same old tricks.

"We walked behind the pool and there were about three couples making out. It looked just like the TV show *Happy Days*, at Inspiration Point. We walked for a while along the path next to the creek. The stone wall was not too tall; it was about knee high. We stopped and sat on the wall in the backyard of one of the houses in the area. Nobody noticed we were in their backyard.

"Michael told me how pretty I was, and that he liked me. I said, 'Thank you.' And here comes the disgusting part—he made a motion with his hand for us to do it. I had no idea what the hell he was talking about," I said, quickly putting my hand over my mouth. Dr. Brown raised one eyebrow at my curse word, and I looked down and said, "Sorry." I then continued my story, "Well anyway, I got mad, jumped up, and said '*No way!* What is this, some kind of science project or something?' I also slapped him, and then I walked away.

"Michael just stood there a second and then yelled, 'Emily, wait!' He didn't want the kids at the pool to think his date went bad. So he talked me into walking back with him to the pool. I did. The kids were still in the same places making out. Then I got away from Michael and went swimming.

"Shortly before school started, almost a week or two after this happened; I went to visit Grandma Washborne. She lived in Morrisville in a house in the university area. She's still there. Grandma is pretty easy to talk to.

"We had long, long conversations about everything, including boys. Because I would have looked like a whore to my grandmother, I added a few things that were not true when I told her about what Michael wanted to do to me. She just wouldn't understand why I was alone with a boy. I lied and told her he had a knife, but he really didn't.

"My grandmother decided to tell my father when he came to pick me up. He went straight to the outdoor pool the next chance he had. I remember him telling me to wait for him before going into the girl's changing room. He went over to Michael and sat real close to him. I saw him lean right up to his ear and talk to him; it was shorter than five minutes. From that day on, I had no contact or conversations with Michael ever again.

"Dad thought he needed to talk to me about this situation. But he was a young dad and didn't know what to say to let me know I did the right thing. I'll tell you what he told me, but it's going to sound really weird.

"I went into the front living room of the house on Park Street. There was a foyer at the front of the house, a living room that children were not allowed to be in, a dining room that we only ate in on Sundays or holidays, the kitchen, and then the family room. We all watched TV together in the family room. But the living room was for adults; it was not for children.

"He sat me down and said, 'That thing Michael wanted to do with you is how babies are made. Young girls who can't afford their babies smother them with pillows and put them in garbage cans.' That statement sort of puzzled me, but I didn't give it much thought after he said that. It really didn't bother me too much.

"My father also showed me how to kick boys where it would really hurt them, in case I ever found myself in a position I didn't want to be in. This was very interesting to me, and I was glad he told me that part.

"When the summer before sixth grade was ending, Mom decided to move us again. This time we moved to a country house in a very pretty and small place called Hartville. I think Mom moved us out there because the rent was cheaper, and she struggled financially. Also, the school district in Hartville merged with Waterville. Mom wouldn't have moved anywhere that we had to change schools.

"The country house was cute. There was a big apartment downstairs, but it was empty. My sister and I each had our own bedroom. Mom slept in one of our beds when we went to school. She still worked the night shift for the hospital.

"Sixth grade was very different than fourth and fifth grade. Now that Hartville students were combined with Waterville, the special education classes got bigger. Mrs. C. still taught a third—and fourth-grade combination class. There were now two fifth—and sixth-grade combination classes.

"I loved school. My favorite subject was English. I also liked math and social studies, but science was really my worst subject. The new science teacher, Mr. H., didn't really teach us; he just handed us packets of projects and expected us to know what to do. He would stand around in the classroom and just supervise.

"Mr. H. was funny looking, too. He was medium in height and really skinny and he wore really tight pants. He had dark black hair in a hairstyle like the 1950s, and he had dark brown eyes. His face was pale like my mom's, only with dark features.

"Anyway, he didn't make science fun or exciting, so I didn't do very well in his class. Sixth grade went by very fast.

"My mother kept in touch with her friends outside of Oxford: Andrea and Jack. They were married and had a baby girl. We were two hours away, and Mom missed her friends a lot, so after sixth grade, Mom decided to move us again. Then—"

"Emily, sorry to interrupt, but our time is up," Dr. Brown said.

"Okay, see you in a week, right?"

"Yes, see you in a week. And have a good one," Dr. Brown said.

I left the office, found Julie in the waiting room, and we got in the car to head home.

When Julie and I got in the car, another popular song was on. This particular song seemed very fitting for how I felt about my father. It was "Cats in the Cradle," by Harry Chopin. Dad really didn't balance having two families well. It was very difficult for my sister and I; we often felt like he chose his second wife and her children over us. They grew up in three different houses, and they had everything. They went on vacations, and it appeared as though they had so much more than my sister and me. My mother really struggled to provide for us.

Another week went by, and I was on the way to therapy when another great song came on the car radio: "Summer Breeze" by Seals and Crofts. This was very ironic because when I talked to Dr. Brown, I was still talking about summer.

"Well, I hope you laugh because I have one more boy story to tell you," I began. "Okay, we moved to a nice apartment back in Oxford. I was thirteen years old and very boy crazy.

"Justin and I were best friends in third grade. We were inseparable, like peas and carrots. He even came to one of my birthday parties. We were both the big mouths of third grade. He had a stepmom, brother, sister, and little half-sister, so his family was similar to mine.

"Justin had brown hair and blue eyes; he was kind of husky but wore nice clothes. We were about the same height. Anyway, before I even started seventh grade, he came over to our new apartment to welcome me back to Oxford. We talked on the phone a few times and then set a date to see each other. I rode my bike to meet him at the outdoor pool. Before we went swimming, he wanted to go for a walk. I wasn't thinking about his raging hormones; I was thinking this was my friend from third grade.

"I was wrong," I confessed, looking down at my feet. "We were walking along, and we found a space to put our towels down. Justin wanted to stop to sit down for a few minutes, and he also wanted to make out. I had no experience at all with kissing. I only saw kissing on TV and had kissed my parents good night. Other than that, my impression was to pucker my lips and keep my mouth closed.

"Well, Justin had something else on his mind. He was all over me like a nasty dog. He put his mouth over mine, and it was wide open. He was trying to stick his tongue in my mouth, and it was wet," I said with a giggle. "Then we stopped. He turned to me and told me he wanted to do it," I paused, sighing. "Only this time, because I was thirteen and a young lady, I knew I was too young and wasn't going to do it. So, I yelled '*No way!* It's kissing or nothing!'

"Well, Justin didn't take this rejection very well. He got mad and no longer wanted to make out. We didn't go swimming together after we got up off the towels, either. He went his way, and I went mine. We didn't talk much after that," I took another moment to pause and collect my thoughts. "That's all the boy stories, I guess, until I get older."

I switched topics and decided to tell Dr. Brown more about school. "Last year, I went to the Oxford Junior High for seventh grade," I said. "I did pretty well, except for science again. I wanted to go live with my father and his new family. Mom told me that part about my Dad not loving her. On top of that, this year we had those stupid photo cubes to get together with the pictures of when we were babies. I just couldn't bring myself to bother Julie with the past. So, here I am. Now that I've lost my head, I'm out of school for a while. I embarrassed my father and his new family." I looked up at Dr. Brown and said, "I have a question for you."

"Okay, what's that?" he replied.

"I guess Mom has been seeing Tom since the summer, and she moved to Hamilton. They are getting married in March, and I don't want to live with my father anymore; I want to move back with my mother. What do you think?"

Dr. Brown scratched his head and looked surprised. He then said, "I don't know, you'll have to ask your mother when you see her. Are you going to see her for Thanksgiving?"

"Yes," I said, filled with visions of a golden turkey and warm apple pies.

"You ask your mother, and see what she says. Also, do me a favor?"

"Sure, anything."

"Don't tell your father that you want to move back with your mom," the doctor advised. "After she gives you an answer, I will have a meeting with your father and tell him, okay?"

"Yeah, sure. I can do that."

"Emily, next Monday I won't see you. And the following Monday is the week of Thanksgiving, and I will be out of town. I won't be seeing you until the following week: Monday, December 3. You will be fine, and I look forward to seeing you then. Make sure you tell Julie, okay?"

"Yes, I will. I will tell her that I won't see you for three weeks because of the holiday and your vacation," I said.

I went out to the waiting room and told Julie Dr. Brown wouldn't be available for the next couple weeks.

"Emily, we should change the time of your appointments from morning to late afternoon; you'll be back to school by then, okay?" Julie said. She made the next appointment for Tuesday, Dec. 4.

Chapter 6

Moving back to Mom's

The next three weeks seemed to be very, very long. I was snapping back to my old self, but there were side effects from the medication I was taking. I was not able to cry; the tears just wouldn't come. I was often sleepy, and my mouth was very dry. Sometimes I would be sitting with my mouth open and not even realize it. My father would stare at me with his mouth open as a reminder. I also always felt like I wanted to walk around, especially when I was in the car. If I was traveling for a long time; it was like the ants were in my feet.

Mom came to pick me up on a Wednesday at 4:30 PM. She was by herself and told me my sister had stayed home. I put my suitcase in the car, got in the front seat, fastened my seat belt, and started talking right away. I didn't waste any time asking her if I could move in.

"Dr. Brown told me to only ask you and not to mention this to my father or Julie: I want to move back in with you, Connie, and Tom."

Mom hesitated for about thirty seconds, and it felt like the longest thirty seconds of my life. After the awkward pause, she said,

"Let me discuss it with Tom, and I will let you know before I bring you back to your father's, okay?"

"Yes, Mom. Thank you."

We had a great time during that Thanksgiving recess. We had a wonderful dinner one night where we laughed and told jokes, and we played poker with pennies at my grandparent's house another evening. It was a great time.

On the way back to my dad's, Mom said Tom thought it would be no problem for me to move back in with them. I would just have to wait until they moved into a three-bedroom townhouse.

On December 4, I returned to Dr. Brown's office. After being escorted in, he asked me, "Well Emily, how was your Thanksgiving with your mom and family?"

"It was good. Do you want to know what my mother said about me moving back with her, Tom, and Connie?" I asked.

"Absolutely. Go ahead."

"Mom said she talked to Tom about it, and he agreed that I can come back," I said with a wide smile. "The only thing is I have to wait until they get a three-bedroom townhouse; I don't know when that will be," I paused, looking down at the floor. "So what will you do now?"

"Don't worry, Emily. I will call your dad, have a meeting with him and Julie, and let them know it's in your best interest to return to live with your mother. I will also tell them you've asked your mom already."

"Okay, thank you."

"Tell me about school," Dr. Brown said.

"Okay. I went today, and it's hard. I went to all my classes and everyone was glad to see me. One of my friends is Madeline; she is in most of my classes. If it weren't for her, I don't think I would be able to stay in school," I admitted. "I don't know what happened to Daniel, he's not there anymore. I think his family moved away."

"What do you think of Daniel now?"

"I'm hoping I'll see him one more time. I want to apologize for how we ended things, and I want to say, 'Goodbye.'"

"What do you think he would say?" Dr. Brown asked, stroking his chin with his fingertips.

"I think he would want to know that I'm okay, back in school, and have my head back. I don't know what my father told him, though."

"What else is going on in school?"

"In Band, I play clarinet. I was first clarinet and third best player of the group of about twenty clarinet players. We had playoffs yesterday. That's where each player plays a song alone so the teacher can see how well we're doing. If someone doesn't play well, they can lose their spot. I don't play as well now that I'm back. After I played my song alone and the results were in, I got knocked down to first clarinet and eighth chair. It hurt a little because I love my clarinet, and I love music. The rest of my classes are fine. We're not doing early child development in Home Economics anymore, thank God!" I said, letting out a huge sigh.

Dr. Brown smiled and said, "I bet you're glad about that."

"Oh yeah, I don't want to have to go through that again! We are sewing now, and Julie just happens to be very good at sewing. She can sew, and I am in great need of help with my skirt," I admitted. Then I changed the subject to what was really on my mind. "Well, Christmas is coming, and I'm going to my mom's again. When do you think you'll talk to my dad?" I asked.

"I don't know. I'll give him a call later, okay?"

"Yes, thank you. That would be great."

The session was almost over, and the doctor and I made small talk to finish off our time together. Usually all Dr. Brown could muster was, "Uh-huh, what else?" But this time he really asked more in-depth questions. All in all, it was a pretty good session.

Later in the week, my father had a meeting with Dr. Brown. Dad's heart was completely crushed when he found out what I'd planned behind his back. And I'm sure the worst part was that he had to hear it from Dr. Brown. The tension was considerably high at my father's house for the next five to six weeks.

Christmas came and went. I continued to see the doctor, except I was seeing him bi-weekly now instead of weekly. I was doing okay in school, but getting very anxious about leaving for Morrisville to start a new life. I could also feel the emotional stress my dad was under at the thought of me leaving to live with my mother.

I moved to Morrisville in January 1980. The townhouse was very spacious, and I had my own room. Connie was glad to see me, but not too glad. Tom acted like he was happy I moved back, but I felt a little rejection. If he was really happy I moved back, why did he give all his attention to Connie?

Maybe it was because I was so demanding of attention from others—good or bad. He didn't know how to react to me sometimes. He did the best he could. I never cared about how Connie felt about my behavior or choices at the time, though.

My mother worked the night shift at the hospital, and it felt like Mom and I were alone in the house. It seemed like Tom and Connie didn't have anything to do with us.

I started school that Monday in the new school district. I was taking basic classes, but it was hard to focus. The district didn't offer me a resource room or any extra help. I was a little shy and didn't make friends right away. I did, however, meet a boy named Barry in my math class.

Dr. Brown had an office about thirty minutes away from where Mom and Tom lived, which was very convenient. The office was in a Fayetteville, where a lot of rich people lived, and it was a long but pleasant drive. I had an appointment a week after I started school.

The office was very nice compared to the clinic where my father lived; it had expensive-looking furniture, and everything seemed tidy and clean. When it was my turn to go into the office, Dr. Brown came out and invited me in.

When I walked into the room, I said, "*Wow!* This is really nice!" The chair I sat in this time was not one you would find in a church basement; it was a leather lounge chair, and it was very comfortable.

We talked for a while about school, and then I mentioned Barry. "He is tall and cute, he has braces on his teeth, and he is Irish. He has a pale complexion, hazel eyes, brown hair, and he is very neat in his appearance. He walks up to me every single day in our math class to ask me the same questions."

"What does he ask you?" the doctor asked.

"He asks how my sister is, and he asks if I have any gum or candy. Why he's asking for candy and gum with braces, I'll never know. It's kind of annoying, though, that he always asks me about my sister. It's like he's trying to make me jealous or something.

"He has three older sisters; he is the only boy. In fact, his name was going to be Emily if he had been a girl. He told me that he was a surprise, like a change-of-life baby; whatever that means. We became instant friends and have exchanged phone numbers. "There's this soap opera on TV that we both watch faithfully. Then at 4:00 PM there's another half hour show that we both watch, and at exactly 4:30 PM every day, I call Barry or he calls me. Then he has to cook dinner for his family, and they eat at exactly 5:45 PM every night."

"This seems like the beginning of a very interesting relationship," Dr. Brown said. "So, do you like him a lot?"

"Yeah, Barry's cute, and we are really good friends. We are sweethearts, actually. We're going to see each other this weekend; we're going to the mall to window-shop or something."

"That sounds like fun," he replied. As a matter of fact, Dr. Brown seemed to turn what I said around a lot; he often repeated what I said and put "it sounds like" in front of it.

The session went well. Mom and I went home, and life went on. Every day was a little more boring than the day before.

Mom was taking parenting classes called S.T.E.P., which stood for Systematic Training for Effective Parenting. She learned from the class that there are four major causes of misbehavior in children and adolescents: displaying inadequacy, power, revenge, or attention. I made some bad choices while I was living with her this time, and Mom decided to finally enforce consequences for them.

One bad choice she never caught on to was how I used to treat our cat. I mauled Jim Bob, our fat cat who didn't like to be held, until he would growl at me. Then I would throw him down the stairs as hard as I could. I never talked about this cruelty to animals to anyone.

I made crank calls to restaurants and made false reservations. I also ordered pizza, sending it to other people's houses. And because one of the houses I ordered for was my Granny C's neighbor, I got caught. Mom grounded me from the TV, the phone, and my stereo for four weeks. This was too much for me to accept, so I decided to do something about it. I was so used to Mom caving in and giving me my own way, maybe this idea of mine would make her give me back my privileges.

It was a Sunday in April, and I decided to take a bunch of pills that I'd found in the house. I took a bunch of aspirin, vitamins, Tylenol, and whatever else I could find. I took about thirty pills in total. Then I wrote a note and left it on the floor in front of Mom and Tom's bedroom. I went to my room to lie down and waited about thirty minutes. Tom had not gone to bed yet, so he still hadn't found the note. I started to get nervous, but I waited another ten to fifteen minutes. Then I got out of bed, grabbed the note in front of their door, went downstairs, and handed it to Tom. He took the note and ran upstairs, waking up my mother to show it to her.

Mom called poison control and took me to the hospital. The nurses made me drink ipecac so I'd throw up the pills I had swallowed.

We returned home, and I missed one day of school. I asked if I could have my privileges back, but Mom refused. I was not happy with that answer, so a week later, I overdosed again.

It was the Sunday after the first overdose, and my mom was doing laundry in the basement. I took the keys to the locked filing cabinet, opened it up, and took out Tom's asthma medication. I hid it under my bed and swallowed every pill before I went to school the next day.

After about half an hour, I started to feel a little shaky. Mom questioned me a little in the morning, asking me if I did something I shouldn't have. I told her I did not. When I got to school, my heart was pounding really fast. Finally, I couldn't stand it anymore; I went to the nurse and told her what I took. The nurse called up my mother, looking at me while she spoke. The nurse was staring at me intensely, like she was waiting for me to explode.

Mom came to school and took me to the hospital. She was absolutely silent during the drive, knuckles white on the wheel, staring straight ahead. This time, I had heart monitors hooked up to me at the hospital. I had to drink ipecac again, but I also had to wash it down with charcoal this time. I was in the hospital all day. Mom was on the phone and left me in the room alone more than she was with me.

That's when Dr. Brown had me admitted to a combined adolescent and adult psychiatric ward in a nearby hospital. This seemed like a real treat to me because there was a TV, a piano, a pool table, and a ping-pong table on the ward. I could stay up as late as I wanted and there weren't too many rules to follow.

The psychiatric ward was fun at first, but it got boring after about two weeks. The adult patients were all either really boring or really screwed up in the head, so there was no one to really talk to or be friends with. I played the piano and watched TV, but I was still bored. At the end of my twenty-day stay, I was ready to go home but didn't really have a clue as to why I was there in the first place.

The school district, however, didn't want me back in regular school. They had me go half a day and see one teacher in the library to finish out eighth grade. I didn't care, because I got to ride a small bus to school. I rode with the half-day kindergarteners, and I always wanted to be a kindergarten teacher. The kids on the bus liked me; we sang songs, and it was so much fun to be with five—and six-year-olds twice a day.

The summer came and, once again, I was bored. I didn't play sports, and I didn't play clarinet in the band at school anymore.

Instead, I would listen to music, talk on the phone, and watch TV. I was home most of the time.

There was a swimming pool at the complex where my family and I lived. Barry met me a few times at the pool, but it had been a cool summer so far; there hadn't been a lot of days to go swimming. I was so bored. We went exploring in the area. There was some land near the railroad tracks that was not developed yet. There was a lot of farmland, a couple of abandoned farm buildings, and abandoned houses.

I watched TV a lot that summer because there wasn't anything to do when I wasn't with Barry. I didn't like being outdoors alone. I gained weight from being on the anti-depressants. One day, while watching reruns of my favorite shows, I saw a commercial advertising a helpline. It looked pretty cool because no one could tell my mother or anyone I knew what I said to the person on the other line.

My mother accused me of eating marshmallows one day that summer, but I honestly hadn't eaten any. I was telling the truth, but because I was a known liar, my mother didn't believe me. I decided I was going to run away. I was going to find a payphone and call that helpline number I saw on TV.

I packed my knapsack with underclothes and a couple of outfits, and I set my alarm clock for about 5:00 AM. I got up when the alarm went off, grabbed my knapsack, and left the townhouse. I walked to the nearest payphone, which was almost a mile away. I had a dime for the phone call, but when I picked up the phone it was out of order. I had to turn around and go home. I never told my mother about my attempt to run away.

September could not come soon enough. I was seeing Dr. Brown every three weeks now. I gave him a recall of the weeks since our last meeting and usually wrote down what I wanted to say so I didn't forget anything.

The school district had decided to put me in special education classes. I was getting a label: I was now "emotionally disturbed" (even though the district didn't do any testing or have an official evaluation). Instead of cooperating, I picked up some bad habits and was a little rebellious. I emulated one of the bigmouth girls in class. She was obnoxious and used bad language. I didn't have consequences at home if I acted up in school, so I copied her bad behavior. I still loved school, but it was boring, and I lost my desire to do well.

I never really had any female role models in my life, so it was hard to imagine what direction I wanted for my life or what directions were even possible. I was very consumed with fantasy, and the soap operas were not helping. I spent an incredible amount of time with Grandma Washborne, a retired English teacher, and I idolized her. I wanted to be a teacher like her. I loved young children and was great at being creative around small or large groups of kids.

School sucked. I was fifteen and very obnoxious. The bigmouth girl in class would make fun of me because she caught me picking my nose once. And I missed Barry; he didn't go to my school anymore because he was sent off to a Catholic high school.

At first, I had a full schedule: Spanish, English, gym, science, and social studies. I followed that schedule for about two or three weeks, and then it got to be overwhelming. The school changed my schedule so all my classes were in one room. I didn't have to take Spanish anymore, but I had gym every day.

I started talking to a new boy in class named George. He had just transferred from a residential school in Buffalo; it was a place where you could go to school and live right on campus. It was kind of like living in a college dorm, except it was all girls or all boys. There were lots of rules to follow, he said, and you couldn't leave when you wanted to. I asked Annie, the bigmouth, how I could get sent to a school like that and live away from home.

She suggested I make up a horrific lie about wanting to hurt someone in my house. I would be sent away for sure. So after Thanksgiving that year, I told Dr. Brown I wanted to do something violent to Tom. This got all the adults in my life busy; they all began searching for a residential facility for me.

My mom and I visited a school close to Pennsylvania. It was okay, and the girls there were nice, but the adults were looking specifically for a residential facility that would better meet my educational and mental health needs.

The appropriate place for me was apparently the same place George told me about. Dr. Brown and my mom submitted the paperwork, and I rode to Buffalo to have an interview. A phone call came about ten days later saying I had been accepted; my moving date was February 11, 1981.

I saw Dr. Brown for the last time the day before I left for the facility. It was the usual forty-five minute ride to the suburb. I made a list of all the things I wanted to talk about. I only had enough to say for half the session, though. "Well, I'm leaving tomorrow for the residential school," I began.

"How are you feeling about that?" Dr. Brown asked.

"Well, I like moving because I'm so used to it. I especially like starting all over again. This place is very pretty, and it's big. It even has an indoor swimming pool, and everybody there is very nice."

"That's good," Dr. Brown responded.

"I'm gonna write everybody. I will write you and let you know how I am doing."

"That would be very nice."

We both stood up, and I gave Dr. Brown a hug before leaving. When my mom and I got in the car, "Turn! Turn! Turn! (To Everything There is Season)" by the Byrds was playing.

I had packed everything I thought I needed for the move. I just had to put out my clothes for my first day at the residential school. A woman from social services was picking me up to take me there in the morning.

Chapter 7

Welcome to the System

I woke up early in the morning as planned, in good spirits and ready to go. I didn't know how Mom was feeling, and I didn't care. I was greedy and selfish at the time, and I did some pretty awful things to get attention.

In the car, I talked to the woman from social services non-stop, all the way to Buffalo. It was a nice ride, and she didn't drive too fast.

The first cottage I was sent to was Herbert; it was where everyone went when they were first coming in and being processed, and it was the only cottage that had boys and girls together. There was a mixture of nationalities in the cottage, including black staff and black residents. I never had any black friends before. Both of my grandmothers gave me false information for the first fifteen years of my life about people who were not the same skin color as me.

Grandma Washborne would send mixed messages about black people. One minute she would complement her black students, and another minute she would make racist remarks because of all the bad experiences she claimed to have had with black students. With

Granny C., there was no flexibility at all. She was Irish, and she always thought negatively about black people.

I spent the majority of my weekends, school vacations, and summers with these two women. And before I moved to the residential school, I was a racist just like they were. But I soon found out how wrong my grandmothers were. In my first week or so at the cottage, my life was no longer white and prissy. I decided not to be a racist anymore.

I promised myself after spending time at the cottage that if I ever had children, they would be around a mix of cultures; they would never be secluded from people of another skin color.

After two weeks at the school, there was an opening at Franklin cottage for me. The staff supervisor at Franklin was Mr. Cole. He was a tall, skinny blonde, and he was very nice. Everyone on the staff was warm and welcoming, and the residents addressed the female staff as "Miss," followed by their first name. Miss Doreen was very cool; she was a single black woman with no kids, and she was so nice. I trusted her. I felt like I could tell her anything.

I had gained a lot of weight in the previous year. It was a combination of over-eating unhealthy foods and the medication I was on after my nervous breakdown. There was a main kitchen in the facility that sent food over to each cottage, and the employees knew the school had me on a diet. This was not fun for me, and a black student named LaTeshia made fun of me relentlessly for it.

She would make fun of me at mealtime, whenever we were in the dining room. We didn't sit at the same table, but we made eye contact every single breakfast, lunch, and dinner. When students got pudding for dessert, I ended up with JELL-O—without whipped cream on top. LaTeshia would take a spoonful of her pudding, start to put it to her mouth, and moan in delight at whatever she was eating. She would make loud noises and dramatize how delicious her dessert was, staring at me the whole time because she knew I wasn't getting any.

I was a drama queen and took LaTeshia making fun of me way too seriously. I remember being upset about the "Wilbur" nickname when I was in third and fourth grade, but the kids got tired of that name-calling, eventually. This girl, on the other hand, was just way too much. She made it her daily personal goal—every waking moment we were together—to make me cry.

I was able to go to Hamilton on home visits, which was so much fun because I rode the Greyhound bus by myself, and Mom picked me up at the bus station. I would get in around 5:10 PM on a Friday afternoon, and I would leave early in the afternoon on Sunday.

I didn't talk to strangers too much on the ride home, because there were some creepy people, and I had to be careful. But I would sometimes find a young, friendly female to make friends with for the ride.

When we arrived at the station, I was not good at avoiding the vending machines. They were almost impossible to resist with all that junk food, especially when I had money.

I left for my first home visit on a Friday in March, shortly after moving into the residential home. Mom was going to let me see Barry, and we had planned a roller skating date. We were going to the popular skating rink in town, which was always something to look forward to.

On Saturday night, my mom picked up Barry and took us to the skating rink. She dropped us off, and we went in, paid, and put our skates on.

I was pretty good at roller skating back then. I learned to skate when I was about seven years old, and Mom used to take Connie and me roller skating every other weekend. Sometimes when we visited my grandparents, they would go roller skating too. Granny would just sit and watch, but Grandpa would get right out there and skate. The last time Grandpa went roller skating with us, though, he broke his elbow.

Barry could skate well, too. We got kind of bored after a few laps on the rink and decided to go outside. We had lockers for our stuff, and it was only a quarter to lock up our skates and personal belongings while we went outside. There was a school with a playground behind the roller rink. We went over to a round ride called a merry-go-round. Whoever got on the merry-go-round had to manually run around it to make it spin, and then they'd have to try to jump on.

Barry and I saw how the soap opera actors would kiss on TV, and we wanted to copy them. We gave it our best try right on the merry-go-round. It must have looked pretty funny to an outsider, watching two teenagers spin around and around on this ride while trying to hug and kiss each other without falling off.

When we were finished, we got off the ride and started walking toward the building. We stood behind the building, in the corner where no one could see us. I was about five foot ten and Barry was at least six feet tall, so our height was perfect for an innocent kiss. It was just a smooch, with no tongue action or anything.

It was okay for me, but Barry was on the blunt side and told me I had bad breath. I wasn't really offended because kissing with my mouth closed felt good for now. We stopped for a minute, and then he showed me with his finger that he was sexually aroused. I knew body parts, and I sort of knew what happens in that situation. But even at almost sixteen, I was a little dumb in that department.

It was cold outside, about twenty degrees, and we decided to go back into the roller rink and skate until my mom came to pick us up.

Sunday morning came quickly, and I got my stuff ready to head back to the bus station.

I went back to the school, and I was really very upset. Miss Doreen was working when I got back. I went to the door and insisted on sitting down and talking to her. She looked at me funny, sensing something was wrong.

I looked at her, playing with my fingers and barely able to catch my breath. I nervously said, "I think I'm pregnant."

She was very sensitive while listening carefully to my explanation. I told her what Barry and I had done on the playground and what he showed me with his fingers. Then the tears came. The tears turned into uncontrollable sobbing—mucous streaming out of my nose—because I was really, truly scared.

Miss Doreen looked at me, her hands on my shoulders. She calmly asked me, "Did you have your clothes off?"

"No."

"Well, did he . . . you know?" she asked.

"No," I responded, pretending to know what she meant.

Miss Doreen looked down at the desk and handed me some tissue. In a very caring voice, she said, "Emily, if you didn't have your clothes off and he didn't—you know—then I don't think you're pregnant, okay?"

"Okay, I understand," I said.

I eventually calmed down, blew my nose, got up, and left. I trusted Miss Doreen and didn't worry about it again.

I had been going to a ninth-grade class in the basement of the Georgetown cottage on campus, since the campus at the main school building didn't have any room for me. There were about seven other students in the class with me, and they all lived off-campus in Buffalo. I was the only student in class who lived at the school.

We learned social studies, English, and some math in the class, which was taught by Mr. Mack. We didn't have science, thankfully, and we went on field trips two to three times a week. I never had homework, and the kids in class were okay.

In the middle of May 1981, there was an announcement made that the school was overflowing with female residents. There was now a great need to have two cottages for girls. One cottage would be for preteens or young teenagers. The second cottage—where I would be placed—would be for older girls: teenagers who needed to learn independent living skills.

At Franklin cottage, we had used a "step" system with points. During each eight-hour shift, our behavior was judged. If we misbehaved, we got a check, and if we were good, we didn't get any. There were five levels students were placed in based on this rating system: extended honors, regular honors, group I, group II, and cottage. Cottage level was the bottom of the totem pole with an 8:00 PM bedtime. Residents in the extended level were allowed walks off campus alone for an hour or two each day.

I worked hard sometimes, but other times my mouth got me into trouble. I went back and forth with my behavior and stayed between group I and group II. I had to be very, very careful to avoid being placed in the cottage level after returning from a home visit; the first two eight-hour shifts I was back counted double for the shifts I had missed while I was away.

Mr. Brooks was the new supervisor, and Mr. Bradley was the assistant supervisor of the older girls' cottage. There was also new staff for me to get used to, as well as a new behavior system. This older girls' cottage behavior system was called "specials" not "honors." Instead of checkmarks for when we followed the rules, we got "S's" for satisfactory. When we acted up, we got a "U" for unsatisfactory.

Mr. Bradley was a tall blond with blue eyes, and he was well-liked by the girls. I think about five of us had a crush on him, and we would talk about how cute he was. He was twenty-nine and single.

The summer was hot that year, and the routine at the cottage was quite boring. We continued to go to school after we moved to Skyview, the cottage for the older girls. I shared a room with Sharon; she was okay, but she had a lot of issues that I didn't know about before moving in. She was shy, withdrawn, and insecure. Then there was Megan; we were friends.

One day in late September, Megan told me she had heard the world was going to end. She said a woman from the 1800s made a prediction that the world was going to end at 2:00 AM on Dec. 30, 1980. I actually believed her story. I couldn't process this information I was given, and I started to become very obsessed with this new theory.

Chapter 8

The End of the World

I was an emotional wreck after Megan told me about the world ending. I was shocked, worried, and scared all at the same time. The following weekend, I went on a home visit. I opened my mother's address book and wrote letters to everyone I knew, telling him or her that the world was ending. I had to warn them.

I wrote my cousins, aunts, and uncles. My cousins wrote back for a while and then stopped, but my aunt and I continued to write back and forth.

I changed my behavior in the cottage and at school. My new goal was to get on extended specials—the highest level of privileges. In order to do so, I would have to get "S's" during every shift for six straight weeks. I couldn't get one "U" during an eight-hour shift. This wasn't really hard at all; if I kept to myself and minded my own business, I would be just fine.

LaTeshia still lived in the same cottage as me, and she still teased me most of the time. But I was doing well with losing weight, and I just ignored her. I had been going to the campus gym and swimming laps in the indoor swimming pool. I swam about five to eight laps each time I went swimming.

I weighed 206 pounds when I first got to the school in February. Less than a year later, I was down to 170 pounds. I was getting a little obsessed with my weight, though. I went to the nurse's office before school started, during lunch, and after school. I was not talking to anyone; I just kept to myself.

The staff did not pay much attention to the changes in my behavior. Years later, Miss Clara, one of the staff, told me the others thought I was faking it.

I had a part-time job at the gym, cleaning the gym and pool area. I was saving money for the first time in my life, working two to three days a week for three hours. I still minded my own business and was getting closer to reaching my goal of extended specials.

In September, I started the high school class on the main campus. I was obnoxious, rude, and disrespectful at first. But after about three weeks, I calmed down and had the desire to do better and be respectful. I was fueled by the thought of getting on extended specials.

Mr. Bradley loved disciplining the residents. He would provoke them into being sassy with him, and, in response, he would get physical with them. He would be that way with me too, but I tried my best not to be sassy. I yearned for positive attention. Mr. Bradley and I would have lengthy conversations about how I could change for the better, and he would often say stuff I really didn't understand.

October came quickly, and Halloween was right around the corner. I didn't really celebrate Halloween; I thought it was a waste of time, personally. The girls in the cottage were mean to each other, saying things like, "It's not Halloween yet, so you can take your mask off." I loved candy, but I was on a stupid diet, so I stayed away from the sweets—even when I was unsupervised off-campus with money in my pocket. I was doing well in school, but I was still getting nervous when I thought about the end of the world.

My time at the residential school was coming to an end. I loved school, even though it wasn't challenging. My part-time job at the gym gave me extra money, which I could use if I wanted to take a walk downtown and do some shopping. I went on home visits once in a while to see my family, but I wasn't obligated to. I could stay at school and work if I wanted. The staff was very nice, and it seemed as though they liked and trusted me.

I was feeling isolated by November, and I was slowing down. I got more and more withdrawn. I still thought about the world ending multiple times throughout the day. I kept to myself, and I was still losing weight. Life was pretty good, but I was happy and scared at the same time. I stayed in the small playroom at the Skyview cottage, where I sat in the corner and sang Christmas carols to myself. Everyone pretty much left me alone; I didn't bother anyone and no one bothered me.

My behavior had obviously changed. I had been outgoing and talkative to the staff and my friends, and now I was withdrawn and detached. The staff still didn't pay much attention to my new behavior.

I continued to make frequent visits to the nurse's office to see if I had lost more weight. I looked thinner and got compliments all the time about how much better I looked. I was finally getting positive attention.

I was in the playroom on Super Bowl Sunday when one of my favorite staff, Miss Laurie, came to the door. She saw me staring into space, and she said, "Emily, get your coat on. We are going for a ride. And it's a bitter-cold night, so dress warm."

I got up slowly and did what I was told. I went to the coatroom. I put on my heavy winter coat, my boots, hat, and gloves and told Miss Laurie I was ready to go. We went outside to her tiny Subaru and got in. I remember the roads were packed with snow; it was icy and treacherous conditions for traveling. It was also late afternoon and almost dark out. "Another Brick in the Wall" by Pink Floyd was on the radio.

I don't remember parking or walking into the hospital. I do remember the room they put me in; it was small with two cheap leather couches that were an institutional-looking brownish-yellow color. I think there was a one-way mirror so the doctors could see me, but I couldn't see them. I thought I could hear their deep voices in the other room. I waited for a while, and finally a doctor came in to see me.

The doctor was funny looking. He looked almost exactly like Dr. Brown, except he had glasses and curly hair. He had a mustache, and he wore the same type of clothes Dr. Brown wore. I was a little unsettled about that. He also had a soft-spoken voice—without Dr. Brown's southern accent—and he was really nice and polite. He carried a clipboard, asked me some questions, wrote down some notes, and then got up and left the room. Miss Laurie followed him.

After about twenty minutes of being alone in this small, scary room by myself, Miss Laurie opened the door. She looked in and said, "Emily, I'm going to the cafeteria; do you want anything?"

I replied, "I still have my ring and my watch."

She looked confused, and then she shut the door. Two minutes later, someone turned out the lights. I don't think they did it on purpose. But here I was: sixteen and scared to death that the world was supposed to end and never did. Then this new shrink looked like my first shrink, and then the hospital turned out the lights. Suddenly, I heard a swishing noise coming from the vent in the ceiling.

The vent was slightly open, and there was a very small amount of light peeking through. With the lights out and the swishing noise overhead, I became convinced that the hospital was sucking the air out of the room. Maybe they were trying to kill me because I did something terrible. I was so scared.

I don't remember leaving the hospital, but I remember entering the cottage when I came back. I remember feeling very dizzy. The girls were practicing cheers for cheerleading. The girls who were not on a basketball team were usually cheerleaders. I wasn't a cheerleader or on the basketball team.

Miss Laurie walked me up the stairs to my bedroom. She had me wait there and then brought me back a plate of food. It was a hot dog and potato chips. She sat on the floor, and she had a plate too. I guess I wasn't much of an eater at this point. She acted very dramatic about eating the hot dog. She bobbed her head back and forth and up and down, trying to encourage me to eat. I don't remember if I ate or not.

For the next two to three weeks, I was recuperating from my second nervous breakdown, involving my fear about the end of the world, the incident in the hospital—all of it. I was put on medication called Melaril. For the first week or two, it was a strong dose to get me back to my old self. Mr. Bradley would notice the change in dosage and say something silly about the color change.

I thought the room I was in at the hospital was a rubber room. I talked to my father on the phone, right after I came home from the hospital. I told him I was in a rubber room, but I don't know if he believed me. When I was sick and living with him, he had asked me once when I was acting weird, "Do you want to be put in a rubber room?" Maybe that's where the idea stemmed from.

I had been at the residential school for one year, and I was supposed to be going home at this point. When I started to show signs of getting back to my old self, we had a treatment reevaluation meeting. I requested a move to a group home instead of going home, which was another way of manipulating the adults. Living independently was attractive to me, and I wanted to be on my own.

Chapter 9

Breaking Free

Arlene, my assigned social worker, found two possible places for me to go. One was a group home in a nice neighborhood, and I would attend a suburban school. This was for girls only, and there was not a lot of structure. Unfortunately, though, I couldn't go to this group home; the staff felt I needed more supervision and more structure.

The second residence was a co-ed halfway house that was operated by the Hamilton Psychiatric Hospital. It was right down the street from the hospital that my mom left in the early morning after working the night shift.

I visited the halfway house a couple of times in the summer of 1982 when I was seventeen. After about ten days, the staff made their decision; they called the residential school to let Arlene know they had accepted me.

Arlene thought this place was structured enough, so that's where I was placed. But Arlene didn't realize there were problems in the house: the location was not pleasant, the staff was distant, and the rules were unusually strict. I soon wished I had never moved there.

I couldn't move in until after high school started, though. I was able to stay with my mother, and she drove me to Hamilton High School for the first two weeks. Because I had so many credits, I was able to start school as a twelfth grader. I started out taking eleventh and twelfth grade English and doubled up in physical education, too.

It was a big house with lots of space. The living room was the first room in the house after walking in the front door. There was an arch separating the living room—where the staff had their office—and the dining room. There was a medium-sized kitchen past the dining room and another room off the kitchen that served as a kids' lounge. In this room, there was a stereo but no television. Toward the back of the house, there was a small bedroom.

While I was living in the house, there were five residents: four girls and one boy.

The behavior modification system at the halfway house was nothing like the system I was used to at the residential school. The halfway house had ten "steps." If I made it to step ten, I had the most privileges. I had to get to step five to see my mother alone.

I don't know what the staff was judging me on, but I just couldn't seem to be good enough to earn privileges to see my mother alone.

After about two months of trying really hard to please staff, following all the rules, doing all my chores, going to school on time, and coming straight home on time, I just couldn't seem to make it to step five. So I stopped trying and started rebelling.

When I left the residential school, I was a very well-adjusted and well-behaved seventeen-year-old. But after a short time in the new house, things were starting to fall apart. (I'm not sure what I was thinking, but I craved God while I was at this horrible place.)

The girls in the house noticed my frustration. They suggested I get admitted to the adolescent psychiatric in-patient ward in the hospital. The girls found a razor for me and pretended that I wanted to use it on myself. This was to help me get admitted—and it worked. I was interviewed, made up a phony-bologna story about wanting to slice my wrists, and got admitted to the adolescent psychiatric ward.

I was in the hospital for about twenty days. During my stay, I went to the day school in the facility. I took English and social studies classes, and I got along okay. I was stuck there for almost three weeks because of the razor incident.

I returned to high school and the halfway house the day after I left the hospital. I was supposed to be starting twelfth grade in the city school, after doubling up on classes, but the hospital stay changed all that.

My three-year major in high school was business. Whenever I saw my business teacher, Mrs. Potter, she gave me a big hug. She always seemed genuinely glad to see me. I was an average student, and I didn't apply myself too much, but somehow I was still popular with the teachers. I really didn't have any friends and didn't care too much about what other kids thought of me at the time.

Around Thanksgiving, I stopped rebelling so much and tried to be on my best behavior so I could spend time with my family. My mother wanted me to go to my grandparent's house for Thanksgiving, but I had to bring a staff person with me for a supervised visit.

The staff person assigned to me was Margaret; we worked together on goals and talked if I had a problem. She was a vegetarian, which made things quite complicated for Thanksgiving dinner. But Margaret came to my grandparent's house anyway, and Granny had a separate dish set aside for her.

On a cold morning after an ice storm, as I was waiting for the bus to school, a car stopped, and a woman rolled her window down. She told me the schools were closed for the day due to the weather.

I ran into another resident of the halfway house at the bus stop, and we went back up to the house together. When we got to the door, Norma, the staff person on duty, refused to let us back in. She didn't believe the schools were closed.

The other resident and I traveled back down the steep hill—covered in ice—and walked to the house where the director had his office. We let him know the schools were closed, and he called to verify the information. We went back to the house, and Norma let us in.

Shortly after the incident with Norma, I started to rebel again and started to run away on a regular basis. Even though Thanksgiving went well, I still couldn't be good enough to earn time alone with my mother. I couldn't understand what I needed to do differently to earn privileges. It seemed unfair. Deep down I thought that if I behaved badly, maybe I would get to see my mom more. Maybe I'd be shipped somewhere else that would make it easier for me to see her.

The program rule was to come back to the house within twenty-four hours of leaving, in order to be accepted back as a resident. If I didn't come back, I would be discharged.

I met up with Jeff, who was discharged from the halfway house because he had a drug and alcohol problem. On several occasions, he returned to the house and sexually harassed the staff. Jeff and I kept in touch by phone after he was discharged; we had a thing for each other, so I started to skip school and hang out with him. But even though I ran away, I always came back within twenty-four hours because I had nowhere else to go. I didn't give any thought to the possibility of moving home with my mother and sister. I thought I was on my own, and that was that.

Mom and Tom split up again. They were married for a year before splitting up the first time and eventually getting a divorce. Two years later, they started seeing each other again and got back together for about three years. When I was in the halfway house, they broke up for the second time. I was disappointed about the second split because I thought Tom made my mother happy.

The trick to running away from the house was to leave after staff did their usual checks on the residents. First, I blasted the music on my stereo for a few minutes after staff members were done with their rounds. Then I stuffed my pillows under the blankets on my bed, locked my door, and ran down the back stairs and out of the house. I usually hooked up with my boyfriend, Jeff, and we walked the streets until we found a place to sleep for the night.

Usually I did this on a Friday or Saturday night and then returned on Saturday or Sunday when it was mealtime, just before my twenty-four hours were up. I ran away about once or twice a week, right up until Christmas.

I thought Jeff was cute. He had a crooked nose, long eyelashes, and a high forehead. Before I moved to this halfway house, Jeff was dating one of the other residents, but they broke up after I showed interest in Jeff.

Jeff had an adult friend who lived in a senior complex near the halfway house, and we would hang out at his apartment sometimes. It was small but safe and warm for the wintertime.

In January of 1983, I snuck away from the house as usual and ran away to meet Jeff, but I didn't make it back in time for the twenty-four hour cutoff—on purpose. I didn't want to go back there. It had been four months and enough was enough. So I was now discharged from the program and officially homeless.

Jeff eventually got tired of me and moved on to someone else. We broke up shortly after I was discharged from the halfway house.

Chapter 10

Shelters

That winter was bitter cold. I was no longer a resident of the halfway house and had no place to go. The first place I went to was a shelter for women and children; it was not in a very good area of Hamilton. I took a taxi there, and on my way, the driver was pulled over. The police were looking for someone, but I wasn't sure why. The driver had to get out of his car and sit in the police car, which took an extra twenty minutes—and the taximeter was still running.

I stayed at the emergency shelter for about ten days. During those ten days, I stayed in school and went back to the halfway house to get some of my things. Some of my stuff was stolen out of my bedroom and from the shelter, too.

Joanne, one of the girls in the shelter, actually looked pretty similar to me. We had the same color hair, and similarly shaped eyes and face. Sometimes people would mix us up. I was tall and big and she was short and big, and we wore the same size clothes.

I returned to the shelter around 5:00 PM after school one afternoon and went upstairs to my room to put my schoolbooks down. I noticed one of my dresser drawers was slightly opened.

I came down the stairs and called out for the staff.

One of the workers approached me, asking, "Emily, what's wrong?"

"Somebody went through my stuff and a pair of pants are missing. Where is Joanne?"

"What does Joanne have to do with this?"

"She wears the same size as me, and I want to know where she is and where my pants are!"

"I don't know, and you should change your tone or make other arrangements."

"You've got to be kidding me!"

"No, I think you need to make some phone calls and find another place to go tomorrow. You can't go around accusing people."

"I'm not. I just want to know where she is! She's the only one here who can wear my size. Look at me! Think for a minute! We wear the same size! What would you think?"

"Emily, come into the office, and I'll give you some phone numbers of other shelters. You need to find another place to stay if you can't get along with the other women here. Our shelter is for women and children, and you are single. You really need to find another place."

I went to a shelter just for teens run by the local Salvation Army. The staff was very nice; they were young and very interested in helping the teenagers change their lives for the better.

I met a young man named Jack while we were both staying at the teen shelter. He turned eighteen while he was there, and then he was able to get his own apartment. I thought he was really cute. Jack had a reputation as a player, dating the teen girls, taking them to his apartment, and having sex with them. I had low self-esteem, and I fell for his game. I didn't have any respect for myself at all, and I didn't care what I had to do to get the attention I craved.

A few months prior, Jeff and I tried to have sex. We spent a night in October—before he was kicked out of the house—in the alley outside of the Hamilton Psychiatric Hospital, with our coats as blankets. We didn't have sex, because we didn't know what we were doing.

When I met Jack, though, I thought I was ready to give myself to him. I was two months shy of turning eighteen, and I was still a virgin.

In February 1983, I decided to go over to his apartment. We ate macaroni and cheese, and then we went into his bedroom. I liked Jack a lot, and we decided to have sex. *This is it—I'm losing my virginity,* I thought. Jack had a drawer full of rubbers and pulled one out for us. I had no idea what I was doing. I didn't know anything about foreplay or anything about preparation for sex. I was not relaxed or prepared for what happened next.

We did it, and I think it lasted less than ten minutes. It felt like he was humping me like a dog. Then, all of a sudden, he stopped. It was uncomfortable and meaningless. I guess it was not really worth the effort. Anyway, I was officially no longer a virgin.

I was in four homeless shelters during the span of a few short months, and then I lived with Jeff's adult friend. I took over his bedroom. He knew I was seventeen and never made any sexual advances toward me. He was very nice; he let me use his phone and eat whatever food he had. He even gave me keys to the building to come and go as I pleased. But, because it was subsidized housing for disabled people, I couldn't stay if management were to find out.

Being the talkative girl I'd always been, I made the mistake of being overly friendly with the residents. One of them went back and told management that I was living there. As soon as the building manager found out, my friend got a notice that I had to move out within three days.

By March 1983, I had been homeless for about three months. It was at this time that I moved into a community residence for women sixteen and older. There were thirty bedrooms in this building: ten were for women and up to two children, and the other twenty were for single women. I was pretty happy to have a permanent place to stay.

The staff was cool. There were rules I had to follow, and once I got used to the routine and the other residents, I thought I would fit in very well.

In order to live there, I had to pay rent. My father had been paying support to my mother for me, so he switched over to sending me the money. At first, it was $70 on the 15th and again on the 30th. The rent ended up being $56.79 for fifteen days and $60.58 for sixteen days.

I ended up asking my dad for an extra $5 bi-weekly. It seemed as though having less than $15 twice a month for coin-operated laundry and personal items was not enough to live on, but I did it. I was fortunate enough to receive a generous amount of food stamps. And I didn't have a phone or utility bill; I used a pay phone for phone calls.

I didn't feel bad about asking my father for the extra money, because he never increased the amount of child support he gave my mom for my sister and me over the years. The amount stayed the same, even though my father's income increased substantially. My mother should have taken him to court and requested more child support. He was lucky that she didn't.

The women's residence was on a hill and just so happened to be right across the street from the high school I was attending as an eleventh-grader (after being set back a grade following my hospital visit). I would cut through, go down the hill, and go to school. But I was still unhappy and missed a lot of school. As a result, I didn't get good grades, but I was able to pass eleventh grade.

That summer went by fast, and that fall I attended my last year of high school. Afterward, I had no idea what I was going to do. I didn't have any money management skills. I didn't have any short term or long term goals. The people I was surrounded by were single mothers on welfare and unemployed, and my family did not encourage me to do anything. I didn't have any goals of any kind.

I took more business classes in twelfth grade. I also took a class called Developing Family. It was a really silly class; we had to have a pretend marriage with someone in the class. It wasn't fun or educational for me, because there was an uneven number of boys and girls, so I had to partner with another girl. I thought this was stupid and didn't take the class seriously. I did minimal work and got a passing grade.

I kept in touch with my family, and we spent the holidays together. Then I returned to the residence, and I turned nineteen in April 1984. My mother helped me when she could, sometimes with my laundry and sometimes taking me grocery shopping and loading up on food for a few weeks. I learned to cook hot dogs, spaghetti, macaroni and cheese, Oodles of Noodles, and other simple and cheap foods.

I didn't mind living on my own in the community residence, but it was lonely and boring at times. The worst part was stretching $15 for two weeks at a time; no one bothered to teach me anything about money management. I had also gained all the weight back that I had lost at the residential school.

I still had outpatient "talk" therapy at the psychiatric hospital, even though I was discharged from the halfway house. I went to a male psychologist named Jason at an adult clinic, and he was not very talkative for "talk" therapy. Jason would often do the reflective listening thing and/or paraphrasing whatever I said, just repeating it back to me. He had a quiet and soft-spoken voice and didn't show a lot of emotion.

In 1984, I had been consistent with showing up for appointments to see Jason. He, on the other hand, was typically late to see me. He had the same old sayings every time he saw me: "It's always a pleasure to see you" and "Thank you for coming."

I didn't really care a lot about myself at this time; I thought I was a bad person because of my choices. I didn't think I was smart, and I didn't have any friends. Even though he said the same thing over and over every time he saw me, I believed what Jason said. I didn't realize it was a programmed response to our session ending.

What would he really say to me if he weren't bound by professional ethics? If I could read his mind, he'd probably be saying to himself, "You're such a pain in the ass, Emily! Get over yourself and grow the hell up, will ya?"

Most of the time, we talked about my relationships with men. In high school, I talked about the crushes I had on certain boys and how I tried to get their attention. He was a great listener; he didn't say much back, except to repeat back to me what I said to him. He reminded me a lot of Dr. Brown, except Jason couldn't prescribe anything. Once in a while, I asked him not to say "It sounds like . . ." Then he would just sit there and not say anything.

I graduated from high school in June 1984. My mother didn't have a very nice way of telling me to get a job. She was angry with me for whatever reason, and she said in a very derogatory tone, "Get a job and pay your own way because your father is not sending you any more support money." She probably thought I would take her more seriously if she was blunt and direct, but this was not a pleasant conversation, and I really didn't understand it.

I ended up going to another emergency shelter for the homeless because I thought I was being kicked out of the women's residence. I received quite a bit of graduation money, and without common sense, I didn't set any aside for rent.

This new shelter was for men and women who were going through the outpatient recovery process for drug and alcohol addiction. They also had beds for regular single adults who were homeless. The food at this shelter was wonderful.

I hung out with whatever group of people was around. I met two guys who were staying at the shelter, two friends named Michael and Keith. I ended up going on one date with Michael and then going steady with Keith.

Both were cigarette smokers in their early twenties. Michael was more aggressive than Keith, and we ended up going out on a date for the day. It was the worst experience of my life. I was still immature and would hang out with anyone who gave me attention.

Michael gave me the impression he wanted to go swimming and maybe go for a walk. We hung out one summer day, and he had a very specific plan in mind for the two of us. I was lonely and foolish, so I went with him for a walk. We walked all the way to the university area. The shelter was downtown, and it was about a two-mile walk. There was a park there and woods nearby.

We stopped at the convenience store first, and he bought me a soda. Then we went to the park. We had towels with us because I thought we were going swimming. I also had my bathing suit on. Michael had something else in mind—he wanted to make out. And that was fine until he attempted to go further.

I was not willing or in the mood. I was searching for love and romance, not a quickie in the bushes. But I was not experienced with romantic love. I slept with everyone and anyone. I didn't care about the emotional wounds I could feel later in life from this choice. I wanted to date Keith from the shelter. This particular day, I just wanted to hang out with Michael.

But Michael was not going to stop until he got what he wanted. He looked at me, sighed, and said, "I know; I'll take you somewhere where you'll get aroused." We got up, got the towels, and started walking back toward downtown.

Michael took me to the only pornographic theatre in the area. In the lobby of the porn theatre, there was a glass case full of sex toys. There were about six booths in the back of the theatre. There was an unfamiliar, nasty odor in the place, and I got a creepy feeling while I was standing in the lobby.

Michael bought tokens, and we went into a very small booth. He put a token in the small black and white TV, and a movie came on. This was the very first nasty movie I ever saw. There were naked people, and most of them were men—I never knew the penis could be that big! The women were not too pretty, and I was not impressed at all. The movie consisted of a woman giving a man oral sex. I was disgusted, not the least bit turned on, and this did not really help Michael with his plan.

Michael decided to lock the door to the booth, then proceeded to ask me, beg me, nag me, over and over and over, for us to "do it." I had my bathing suit on, and I really, really did not set out to screw this jerk. After what seemed like an eternity, probably about twenty minutes of his begging, I gave in. It was not pleasant, and it was not fast for me. As soon as it was over, I put my bathing suit back on, and he was ready to run out the door like a sly dog who just got what he wanted.

Michael left the homeless shelter, and I carried on a friendship with Keith. I told him what happened with Michael. Keith and I were intimate after about three weeks of hanging out, and we became boyfriend and girlfriend. We had sex every time we saw each other, and we didn't know much about each other at all. I was on the pill, and the only time we didn't do it was when I had my period. I was very fortunate that so far, with the exception of Michael, none of the guys I had sex with asked me to do anything I didn't want to do.

I was at the homeless shelter for two weeks. During those two weeks, I showed up for therapy appointments with Jason. I was very anxious to see him and talk to him alone for fifty minutes, and I tried very hard to utilize my time well during the sessions.

In July, I went to my appointment, and my mother, someone from the women's residence, and two women from an adult program were in the office. I was quite pissed off that I couldn't see Jason alone. I was stuck having a meeting with a roomful of other people.

I was told in the meeting that I had been accepted into the adult transitional apartment program. I could return to the women's residence, and I was not kicked out. I don't remember how I paid for the last couple of weeks there, but I didn't have to return to the homeless shelter.

Two weeks after the meeting, I moved to an apartment with two other female roommates. One girl was very pretty, but she had mental problems, recently had an abortion, and was unemployed. The other woman was very obese and at a dangerous weight for her health. She was slow and depressed. I only lived in this apartment for a few weeks, because I didn't get along well with either of my roommates. I moved to another apartment, and it wasn't a good match either. Finally, I moved to a third and last women's apartment with just one other roommate. This was the best match for me.

Chapter 11

Peter

I was a resident in the special independent living program, learning the skills required to make it on my own. There was an apartment for staff, where the residents could go and socialize and have individual counseling sessions. The staff was available in person or by phone twenty-four hours a day.

There were also group homes as part of the independent living program. One of the group homes was a big house with eight adults, men and women, living together. Most of the time, participants went to the group home first and then transferred over to the apartment program, but I had already lived on my own at the women's residence. I didn't feel I needed to be in a group home before going over to the apartments. Luckily, the staff agreed.

One of the first times I was introduced to the other residents of the group home was at a softball game. It was then that I thought I had met my soulmate for life, Peter. He was so adorable and had such a spunky personality; I desperately wanted him to be the one. Unfortunately, Peter didn't give me the time of day, so I began to chase him.

Soon after we met, he moved to the apartment program from the group home, and his apartment was under mine. I could hear him when he was home, and I knew when he was not home. I had no clue how to present myself to Peter to get positive attention in search of a decent relationship.

When I was chasing Peter, I was in a steady relationship with Keith and willing to go from one person to the next if that was a possible option for me. And as soon as Peter acknowledged that he liked me and was interested in getting to know me, I was ready to drop Keith.

I didn't know what a healthy relationship was. All I ever talked about, even with Keith, was how much I adored Peter and just couldn't wait to be with him. This probably appeared a little obsessive and crazy.

My reputation at the independent living program was most likely as a girl who was cheap. I was not quiet about having boyfriends and enjoying sex in those relationships. It was not a secret that most of the dates I went on, when I didn't have a boyfriend, ended in sex.

I managed to get a position at McDonald's, about a mile away from my apartment. I walked to work 90 percent of the time.

From September 1984 to about mid-April 1985, I went to work, came home to rest, had therapy once a week with Jason, met with staff at the apartment program as required, and I was working very hard at getting Peter's attention in my downtime—while continuing a sexual relationship with Keith.

About mid-April 1985, I started talking to staff about moving to the next level in the independent apartment program. It was a closer step to moving out and living on my own. I wanted more freedom and less attention from staff, and I wanted to eventually have my own apartment.

I sat down with the staff person I was assigned to and wrote out some personal goals. The staff included dates to achieve the goals, and if I did so by the dates listed, I would be eligible to move to the last level in the program before moving out on my own.

Cindy was going to be my roommate when I was ready to move; she was about sixteen years older than me. I actually knew her; we had gone to the same high school, and my grandmother had been her teacher. We hit it off well, and I thought we would be great roommates.

In the early summer, I finally got Peter's attention. I was tall and pretty, but I was immature, insecure, and used sex to get what I wanted—or at least I tried to with Peter. I didn't know what a healthy relationship was, because I had never seen one up close and personal. Peter was finally giving me the attention I had been trying to get for more than a year, so I broke things off with Keith.

Peter and I had a date in his apartment, watching movies. He was really cool about watching a chick flick, then put in an action film with a little romance in the mix. The apartment was comfortable and nicely decorated. I was sitting on the carpet, and Peter was on the couch. He was stretched out and our heads were near each other. He leaned over, held my face, and kissed me. It felt like my whole life had changed forever.

For the next fourteen days or so, I was his sweetheart. He would meet me at my job and walk me home at 3:00 AM. I would normally take a taxi, but Peter was willing to wait for me to call him, meet me, and then walk me home. If there's such a thing as cloud nine, I was on cloud nine, ten, and eleven. [I can hear the song "I Believe (When I Fall in Love With You It Will Be Forever)," by Art Garfunkel.] But Peter had other plans.

He had been in the group home and independent living program for about a year and a half. He had healed from whatever agony he suffered in his life that brought him to the program. Peter was about two years older than me, and he was not a typical resident of the independent living program.

The typical residents in the program were pretty stuck with their issues; they didn't have any family support, and they were not motivated to continue their education or get any job training. There were about five adults in the program, twenty-two to twenty-five years old. In the two years I was in the program, these five people all received medication and attended psychiatric day programs. They would go off medication, get sick, go in the hospital, get back on medication, and come out of the hospital. This would happen over and over again until they left the program.

Peter, however, didn't want to be stuck in the system. He was very smart and ready to move on and further his education so he could get a job. He visited college with one of the apartment staff. Afterward, he came over to see me.

He ended the relationship. I was sure my life would never be the same, but I was also hopeful that I could keep chasing him even if he went to college. (Song: "Against All Odds," by Phil Collins.) At least for fourteen days of my life at twenty years old, I thought I had found my soulmate. It was so glorious. The best part of our short romance was that as much as I would have done anything to him, for him, or with him, we were not intimate.

Peter left for college at the end of August. I was obsessed with him for several months after he left. I wrote him letters, and when I visited my father, who lived near Peter's family, I called him when I knew he was home from college. He was gracious enough to talk to me, but I really needed to move on.

When Peter and I had our little romance, my roommate Cindy and I would have him and his best friend Matt over. We would order pizza and wings. Matt had a guitar, and Cindy loved to sing, so the four of us would just hang out for a few hours on a Friday night. It was a lot of fun, and it was part of the reason Peter attempted to be more than friends with me.

It was so hard to let him go. He was so funny and so wonderful. I was so crushed when he left. All I talked about for at least six months after we broke up was this great crush I had on this outstanding, lovable, sweet, and handsome man who decided college was more important than being held back in Hamilton.

In early 1986, I decided I wanted to live independently, away from the apartment program.

Peter's best friend Matt was a friend of mine, and we wanted to share expenses and live together as friends. He was tall, handsome, and charming, but sex was not on my mind. Also, Matt was a very private and shy person, and he was not looking for a relationship. We found an apartment and moved in together in February, and we lived as platonic roommates for three months.

I chose to mismanage money and didn't pay bills on time. I still had no self-esteem and continued to look for love from men. I had casual affairs here and there with whomever would go out with me. I was attracted to unemployed smokers, drinkers, and sometimes even drug users.

At the end of May, Matt and I had to vacate the apartment because I didn't pay the rent and had no way to catch up. I moved to a building that was close to the Hamilton Psychiatric Hospital and to downtown. I lived in an apartment on the fourth floor. It was actually more like a boarding house; there were about four to five bedrooms in each apartment. Each person paid for their room, and we all shared the bathroom and kitchen.

My mother didn't like the building I lived in, because she felt there was drug dealing going on. She really had nothing to worry about. I didn't have anything valuable that anyone could steal from me. I also was not interested in doing drugs or selling drugs. Shortly after I moved to this building, I quit working at McDonald's and applied for welfare. I should have had another job to go to before quitting this job, but I wasn't thinking clearly. I was just simply sick and tired of fast food work.

I soon found another boarding house and moved. While I was there, I ran into a man from the independent living program named Brett. He was not a resident of the apartments or the group home; he lived on his own in subsidized housing due to his schizophrenia.

Chapter 12

New Job and New Man

The boarding house was located on the city's west end—luckily, the better part of that side of Hamilton. We all shared a bathroom, and each individual room had a refrigerator and a hot plate. I had a spacious bedroom, but I missed being able to walk to my appointments. Now I had to ride the bus.

I hated the new cashier position I had started at Burger King (I was back to food service because that's what I knew best). When I was working at McDonald's until 3:00 AM, I would walk over to the hospital when my mom was working the night shift, wait until she was done working, and then she would give me a ride home. When I worked for Burger King, though, I didn't see her as often.

One morning, Mom came over and suggested I apply to take a home health aide training. I applied in mid-July and was hired for the training, which started August 8 and ended right before Labor Day weekend. I took my mother's advice, for once, and I didn't have to work in fast food anymore!

During the time I took the training to become a home health aide, the apartment program called and accepted me back. I had to live in the complex where the staff lived and worked until an apartment opened up for me.

The home health aide training was great. I went for twelve days, had perfect attendance, and did average on the written exams. I didn't have a car, but luckily, my assigned patients were in the city and on a bus line. The home care agency also contracted with a taxi company. Sometimes, when I worked odd hours or was scheduled for places hard to reach on a bus line, I took a taxi. The home care agency paid for it.

I didn't have great working habits at the time, because I was immature. I passed the training and everything, but I was very lazy. I hated washing dishes, and I hated cleaning, period. Plus, I was confused about whom I wanted to work with and what I could handle. It was hard to work for male patients, having to see them naked.

I got assigned to some male patients who flirted way too much. I wasn't sure what to do about it at first. I would lose the hours if I complained, and if I didn't complain, I was bothered by it. I had sense enough not to lower myself to flirt back with the patients I was assigned to, though.

From August to November of 1986, I lived at the staff complex with one other roommate. In December, the independent living program had an apartment in a really nice area for us to move to. We were the first two residents to live in the apartment, and we got to pick out all the furniture and all the decorations. There was one bedroom with two beds.

I was dating Brett at the time. He was ten and a half years older than me, with blond hair and blue eyes. His hair was receding, and it looked like he would be bald in about ten years. He was not fat but had a small gut over his belt.

We liked the same music, and I had fun hanging out with him. Brett worked under the table, driving a taxi five days a week for twelve to thirteen hours at a time. He was an incredible bowler in his spare time, with a high average of something like 280. He was a heavy cigarette smoker, and he gambled on horses—that was his true addiction. Brett took whatever money he made driving his taxi to the horse track and gambled until he was broke or won big. During this time, he was on medication for his schizophrenia. Somehow, I just didn't see the mental health issue; he always acted so normal. I also didn't see a problem with the gambling.

Brett had some strange ideas about money, the government, different nationalities, bathing, and women. He thought he would inherit money from his mother's brother, a millionaire who lived in Buffalo. He also had great-aunts who were wealthy, and he thought they, too, were going to leave him money.

Brett thought the government owed him, and he wouldn't tell Social Security that he drove a taxi. He said it didn't make any sense for him to work and make minimum wage, taking home $150 a week and sweating his balls off, when he could declare himself disabled, get SSI with Medicaid, and work under the table. He got a lot more money and lived a lot more comfortably while cheating the system. He said, "You either f*** the system or the system f*** you."

He was a flat-out racist, often making derogatory comments about black people. I didn't pay attention, because I didn't want to argue. We usually didn't talk about it.

Brett was very disrespectful toward women, too; he thought men were superior. He told me, "It's easy: get pregnant, have a baby, and go on welfare." I believed him because when I lived at the women's residence, there were women there who had two kids and got welfare. They had about $100 twice a month to spend on whatever they wanted. They also had food stamps, free medical care, and there were no utility bills at the women's residence.

Brett had body odor but wouldn't admit it. He would always say he didn't want to be in a "pretty contest." Brett also said people in Europe go three months without taking a bath. I didn't listen to his irrational comments. Thankfully, when I nagged him to shower more often, he did.

By March of 1987, I received a notice from subsidized housing that my name had come to the top of the list to get a voucher to pay part of my rent. This was very exciting for me because now I could leave the independent living program once again. All I needed was a signature from my therapist, saying that I was not able to work full-time.

Jason was not too happy about signing the paper for me to get subsidized housing, but he did. I found an apartment in a nice neighborhood in Hamilton. It was a cute one bedroom in a three-family house. There were two single brothers who shared the upstairs apartment, and there was a single woman in a one bedroom in the front of the building. My apartment was on the side of the house; it was very spacious for all my stuff.

I was still dating Brett, and it seemed like we were getting serious. We slept together after about a month, and I actually felt guilty for not sleeping with him sooner. He said if anyone at the Hamilton Psychiatric Hospital found out that we had not slept together, it would ruin his reputation. Another player, but at least we had a good sex life.

I decided to settle for Brett. He was good-looking, nice to me, a good lover, and I thought we could be happy together. He had a high school diploma and an associate's degree in math and science. He wasn't stupid, but he decided to use his mental health condition as an excuse to remain unemployed. His parents didn't instill in him the importance of education and employment. He grew up under the influence of gambling and was taught that it was the best way to make money.

Brett told me that when he had his mental health problem, he cut off his mother, Lucy. He had nothing to do with her until we started dating, then we went over to see her a few times. She seemed to be very nice, but Brett had some bad memories and wanted to continue to keep his distance from her.

Lucy gave birth to him when she was thirty-five, and she complained that she didn't get to vote that year because she was in the hospital. His father was the strong and more stable of the two parents, often spoiling Brett. Brett was twenty years old when his father died, and his world crumbled. He told me he and his mother would physically fight.

One fight in particular led to both being admitted to the psychiatric ward, which led Brett down a path of destruction. He was often going on and off medication, which did not help his mental stability.

During this time, he would keep a job for a few months, then quit and go right back to the hospital. Finally, when a staff person pointed out to Brett that he was pretty stable when he stayed on his medication, he began taking it consistently. This was when he was approved for Supplemental Security Income and moved into his own apartment, gaining some stability in his life.

I met my neighbors—the two brothers—from the upstairs apartment. I made friends with the older brother, John; he was very, very nice. I even broke up with Brett so I could go on a few dates with John.

John had a full-time job at a local hospital. He didn't drive. He was shy and drank beer on the weekends. I really didn't want to be involved with a drinker, because of what I had been through with my maternal grandmother. I was also not used to someone who was employed and just plain normal, with no disabilities.

After a few dates with him, I couldn't handle the beer drinking, so I went back to Brett. About two months later, John moved out of our apartment building and into a building that was closer to where he worked. Soon after, I decided I wanted to live closer to Brett. I applied to move my subsidy to his building. He lived in a downtown high-rise, on the twentieth floor. I moved the first of the year, 1988, to an apartment on the ninth floor of his building.

I changed home care agencies that month to one where my mother knew the nursing supervisor. This agency had more of a variety of cases: they sent some home health aides into facilities, and they also had sitter-companion positions in the hospitals. I was still very new to the field and was very insecure about my abilities.

But I was less lazy in private homes now that I had experience in that setting.

I worked at the state hospital on sitter-companion assignments on the night shift. During this time, I crocheted a lot. My sister announced on Christmas that she was getting married in October 1988. I spent January to July crocheting her an afghan for a wedding present. This afghan was large enough for a full size bed, maybe a little bit bigger. The colors were forest green, navy, gray, and white.

I soon realized I didn't like the new agency I worked for—I was insecure in my abilities and didn't feel qualified enough to work there. I decided to go back to the agency that had trained me. The first agency put up with people not showing up for work; they put up with a lot of nonsense. So, as a person who didn't work very hard, the newer agency was like a real job with high expectations. I knew if I screwed up, I would lose my job. That's why I went back to the first agency.

In August, a position became available at the women's residence where I lived as a teenager. I applied in person for a second job and was hired. It was not as easy as I thought, though; I had to do rounds of the whole building every two hours during a ten-hour shift. I was responsible for signing in visitors and making sure the women were safe.

I was trying to get pregnant by Brett during this time because I wanted to get married, and I knew he would marry me if I were having his child. Unfortunately, I didn't have any friends to share my plan with.

My period was due on Friday, September 2, and when Monday came, I still didn't have it. All the free clinics were closed on Monday because it was Labor Day. On Tuesday, I called one of the clinics and made an appointment to get a pregnancy test.

The girl who was working there didn't take the test out of the refrigerator until right before I got there. When she did the test, it really wasn't accurate; she even said that it started to change to positive at the end, but she read it as a negative.

This young lady also decided to give me a lecture about not being married and that my boyfriend didn't have a job at the time. This criticism, although very true, was not helpful for me. I can understand the facility's position on encouraging adoption and their mission to strongly discourage abortion, but I disagree with giving a lecture pointing out the problems in my life. This was supposed to be a pregnancy test, and this woman's personal opinion got in the way of an accurate test result.

Two days later, I went to a non-religious free pregnancy-testing clinic, and the test came out positive. My expected due date was May 12. I was very excited and scared at the same time. I thought I wanted a family, but I was not sure this was the way to go about having one. I thought I wanted to marry Brett, have a baby, and everything would be okay.

But I was not married yet. I was only a home health aide, barely making minimum wage, and I didn't even have my own health insurance. The father of this baby was unemployed and had no intention of ever getting a job. I was still in therapy at the Hamilton Psychiatric Hospital's out-patient clinic. I didn't have anything stable in my life to justify bringing a baby into my world.

Needless to say, the announcement didn't go over well with my family. Their biggest concern was money and stability. My mother was concerned more with the emotional and residential stability. It appeared as though everybody was against me. I was determined to not let anything or anybody stop me. My mind was made up before I knew I was pregnant.

Chapter 13

Priorities

I found out I was pregnant on September 8 and married Brett eight days later. I gave up my subsidized housing on the ninth floor of Brett's building and moved to the twentieth floor with him.

My sister Connie got married a month after me on October 15. My mother told me not to tell Connie that I got married and was pregnant until after her wedding—it would have taken the attention away from my sister on her big day.

Brett continued to work full-time for the taxi company, and I had my two jobs.

I signed up for The Special Supplemental Nutrition Program for Women, Infants and Children (WIC) while I was pregnant. The program provided nutritional information during my pregnancy, as well as checks once a month for milk, juice, eggs, and cheese. If I had chosen not to breastfeed, WIC would've provided checks to pay the cost of formula. When the baby turned four months old, WIC gave checks for juice and cereal.

It was early November, and my family had not taken well to the fact that I was pregnant and married. They were very unkind with their choice of words for conveying how they felt. The emotional stress I was feeling from the lack of support from my family, coupled with my work as a night supervisor—climbing stairs frequently, which caused stress on my body—led me to experience some spotting. I quit the position.

The doctor ordered a sonogram right away. My mother said, "Some women bleed buckets when they are pregnant and still have healthy babies." I continued my job as a home health aide, where no heavy lifting was involved.

I worked between twenty and thirty-six hours each week. One week, I went to a department store that carried baby stuff and clothes for all ages and put some items down on layaway. I also bought books about pregnancy and early baby care.

I contacted a program through a local agency that offered classes in newborn care for first-time parents. They offered a free class to women, and their partners, in their seventh to eighth month of pregnancy. I signed up to take the classes in April, and I was due the following month.

I also ran into Trisha—a former McDonald's coworker—around this time. We actually lived in the same apartment building. She told me she was happy to see that I was happy. Trisha gave me some great advice that I took seriously and decided to follow: she told me to absolutely make sure I go to all my doctor's appointments—no matter what. This was not easy to follow, because I was typically waiting at my clinic for a half hour to an hour and a half after my scheduled appointment time to be seen by a doctor. But I was going to do the best I could.

Brett stopped working five days a week in December and was only working Sundays and Wednesdays. I wasn't really sure why he changed from full-time to part-time. We got along okay, but sometimes it felt like we were living separate lives.

Brett took his money and bought the newspaper, paid the cable bill, bought his cigarettes, and had $50 to $100 to gamble on a horse race or local college football or basketball. He thought of gambling on the horses as his career. He was not concerned with baby stuff.

I, on the other hand, took my part-time wages from working as a home health aide and did small layaways to buy clothes and baby items. It seemed as though we should have been putting our money together or at least talked about our finances and made a plan.

One day in December, while Brett and I were sitting in the bedroom, we had a big argument. I told Brett that with a college degree, he could do something other than gamble and live off the government. He said getting a job wasn't worth it, because it could not take the place of the money he got for free at the time.

We argued back and forth. I was sitting close enough to him on the bed that he decided to reach over and slap me in the face. I felt a sting on my cheek and left the room. I didn't tell anyone, because I didn't want the baby taken from us. Brett didn't say he was sorry for slapping me; he thought he knew everything, and no one could tell him any different. I wished the government would figure out that he was very capable of working, take away his money, and see what he would do on his own.

I worked because I was raised in a different kind of family than Brett. I wanted to support my family and be a good role model for my child.

I had worked as a home health aide for a woman in her early twenties once. She was blind and in a wheelchair, and she lived in her own apartment. Although she could not walk, she managed to have a part-time job. After assisting the blind woman with her daily living skills, I found it very hard to agree with anyone who said they couldn't work.

I was starting to show by early 1989 and really look pregnant. I didn't have good eating habits and was gaining weight all over. But, even at four and a half months pregnant, I was still working part-time for the home care agency, and I went to all my doctor's appointments.

I had lots of questions when I got to the doctor's office. I always sat down with the nurse for a good half hour and talked her ear off about everything. Some things were not even related to the baby. I think I wore her out, poor girl. She made a call, and I was given a referral for a public health nurse to visit me in my apartment once every two to three weeks.

For one doctor's appointment, I was scheduled for 10:30 AM. Noon came and went, and I was still waiting to be seen by the doctor. I didn't care, because I was so happy to be having a baby. I looked up at the clock in the waiting room, and it was suddenly 1:00 PM. Maybe my doctor went to lunch.

I was finally brought into the room at 2:00 PM. I had to urinate in a cup, get weighed on the scale, have my blood pressure taken, and have the fetal height measured. I waited three and a half hours, and the process was over in ten short minutes.

In March, I was almost seven months pregnant—another ten weeks and I would have a new baby!

Brett and I got into another deep discussion about money. I should've known not to sit so close to him again. This time, he took his foot and kicked me in my back. I still kept my mouth shut because I wanted to keep my baby. Even if I had left Brett, I'm sure my family would've harassed me about being a single mother and wanted me to give my baby up for adoption.

The public health nurse was making regular visits to check in on me. She made a referral, because I talked a lot, for a special caseworker to come and see me. I was actually too old for the program, but they made an exception. This caseworker came to see me within a week or two after Brett kicked me. I told her what happened, and she asked if Brett was going to be a threat to the baby. I assured her that he would not do anything to the baby. That was the end of the discussion.

It was a very busy time for me: I had talk therapy once a week, I saw the public health nurse and the caseworker weekly, went to all of my prenatal appointments, and I was still working part-time.

At all my doctor's appointments, the baby appeared to be healthy. The baby was quite big, so I had more sonograms than normally offered during pregnancy. One of the sonograms showed that we were going to have a baby boy! His name would be Edward Franklin Kendall. I was still gaining a lot of weight, but the baby and I were okay. Brett and I were okay, too, but could have been better.

I met Brett's mother, Lucy, a few more times. She came to our wedding and joined us when we went out to dinner afterward. Lucy was almost seventy and lived alone in a decent area of the city, in a two-family house. She rented the upstairs apartment to her aunts. Aunt June and Aunt Iris were in their eighties and homebound in the winter; in fact, June was too frail and sick to leave the house at any time of year.

I scheduled an appointment for a visiting nurse to see Lucy because I was worried about her health. I hoped she could qualify for some help with personal care and light housekeeping from a home care agency. I was very big in the belly and almost four weeks away from having the baby, so I couldn't help her as much as I wanted to.

The day before the visiting nurse was scheduled, Lucy had a fall outside. Roger and Joyce, a couple who took care of the elderly aunts—bringing food, doing any banking, bill paying, and shopping for them—helped Lucy inside her apartment and helped her to bed. They didn't realize how serious the fall was, and they left soon after.

The next day, around 11:00 AM when the visiting nurse was scheduled, Lucy didn't answer her door. Brett and I were at the house to meet the nurse for her first visit, and we called Lucy's house phone, but there was no answer. Aunt Iris had a key to the house, and we were able to get into Lucy's apartment.

Lucy had been in bed since the day before because of her fall. We called an ambulance, and she was treated for her injuries at a nearby hospital. She had broken her elbow and fractured her shoulder, and she was also incontinent. The hospital told us Lucy couldn't go back to her apartment alone—she would have to sell her house and move into a nursing home.

Brett and I made plans to move our subsidy to a suburban neighborhood after the baby was born; we didn't want to raise a child downtown. We kept in touch with the hospital regarding Lucy's condition. The hospital was not consistent with a discharge plan for her; one week they said she could go home, and the next week they said she had to go to a nursing home. If she couldn't go home, she would have to sell her house and use all of the profit on the cost of a nursing home.

Brett contacted a lawyer to make things clear for everyone. The lawyer drew up paperwork so Lucy wouldn't lose her house.

Brett contacted the housing authority and inquired about finding a two-bedroom apartment for us. We found a place on Brett Lane and decided to move there on June 1, 1989.

My due date was May 12, which fell on Mother's Day that year. I stopped working in the middle of April, right before my twenty-fourth birthday, because I was getting big and uncomfortable. My ankles were swollen, and I didn't sleep well. I had weekly doctor appointments until the baby came. I gave notice to the home care agency and went on maternity leave.

Another week went by, and I had a sonogram to make sure the baby was in the right position. Everything looked fine. The sonogram showed that the baby was at least nine pounds and was in the right position—head first.

On Wednesday, May 17, I was having contractions, and I thought I might have the baby. It was Brett's night to drive the taxi, but he took the time off to be with me, and we went to the hospital.

After getting everything together, driving to the hospital, checking in, and seeing a doctor, I was sent home. The baby was not ready yet. Brett was quite upset that he missed a whole night of work for nothing.

I had another doctor's appointment the following Wednesday, and it didn't go very well. My blood pressure was very high—so high, in fact, that the nurse who took it wouldn't tell me what the reading was. The doctor wouldn't let me walk home to get my bag and go to the hospital. The patient account representative called for a Medicaid taxi to take me directly to the hospital. I ended up waiting for almost two hours for the taxi.

I called Brett to get my bag that was already packed and the baby's bag, too, and meet me at the hospital. After I arrived at the hospital, they had me go straight to Labor and Delivery. They hooked me up to a fetal monitor, and they inserted an IV to induce labor. The baby was not ready yet, so the nurses unhooked everything, and I went to the maternity ward to spend the night. The plan was to restart the induction in the morning.

The next morning, May 25, I was taken to Labor and Delivery. The nurse got another IV going to induce my labor. It was a very slow process, and finally, around 4:00 PM, they increased the medicine to make the labor come faster. I started to have contractions an hour later, and they were painful. My mom had warned me they would feel fifty times worse than menstrual cramps. She was right; they felt like horrible, horrible menstrual cramps. She also warned me about back pain, but I was very fortunate not to experience any.

I had a lot of support from my mother and Brett, and I tried very hard not to complain. My mother complimented me on how calm I was. I wanted to have a baby, so I was able to go through all of the suffering and pain of childbirth.

A few hours later, things started to progress faster. I started to dilate, and at 8:30 PM, I started to feel the urge to push. After I felt that urge, all the cramping of the contractions went away.

I was transferred onto a stretcher and taken into a delivery room about an hour later. I pushed about four or five times; my mother said my face became beet red when I was pushing.

My son Edward was born at 10:13 PM. He weighed ten pounds, ten and a half ounces and was twenty-two and a half inches long. Mom worked at the hospital where I delivered Edward, and she was in the delivery room when he was born. Every time the nursing staff asked the obstetrician a question, all eyes were on my mother, who was off-duty at the time.

The obstetrician was known for his disagreeable bedside manner when delivering babies. He was from a clinic, so the relationship he had with patients was not very personal. My mother knew this was going to be a big baby, and she didn't want me to have a cesarean section.

Edward was quickly taken out of the room after delivery for the usual newborn procedures. I heard Roberta Flack's "The First Time Ever I Saw Your Face" in my head. Edward's nose was cleared out, and he was wiped off. The nurse handed Edward to Brett, and my mother said, "Oh, he looks just like Brett." But Edward had very dark hair just like mine.

I didn't believe that I was going to be allowed to take Edward home from the hospital. All the women I knew in the psychiatric system who got pregnant either had abortions or the baby was taken into foster care after delivery. In the back of my head, because I was affiliated with the psychiatric hospital, I thought someone would automatically take Edward away from me at the hospital. It wasn't until I was putting him into his car seat in my mother's car that I realized I was bringing Edward home.

A week after I had my son, we were moving to a nicer neighborhood with our rent subsidy. At the same time, the hospital was discharging Lucy, and she was going to an adult home. Brett had to speak to his great-aunts about paying more rent so Lucy could afford to stay in the adult home. He also wanted to live rent-free in his mother's downstairs apartment, which was dark and dirty. I wasn't sure it was the best place for us.

We lived on Brett Lane for about five months, and then we moved into Lucy's first-floor apartment. I was Lucy's payee for her Social Security, and I used the money to pay the utilities, the taxes on the house, and some of her bills.

I called the adult home frequently, and we tried to visit Lucy once a week. Her arm and shoulder seemed to be healing well, and she appeared to be happy where she was.

The first ten months of Edward's life was pretty normal. I nursed him for about two months, but it was hard to breastfeed such a big baby and even harder to breastfeed in the summer. He was weaned to formula completely at about four months. Thankfully, Edward was not a fussy baby.

Chapter 14

Leaving Peacefully

From the end of May, when Edward was born, until early July 1989, he woke up every three hours on the dot to eat.

On July 4, we went to the beach. It was a perfect, eighty-degree day—just warm enough for us to enjoy the summer day, with a cool enough breeze to be comfortable for a newborn baby. The sky was blue with a few clouds. After we went to the beach, Edward slept five and a half hours for the first time; I think it was the crisp, fresh air that helped him sleep.

Edward crawled when he was exactly six months old. From six to ten months, he started regular baby foods and some easy finger foods. He had a couple of teeth come in, but teething wasn't too much of a problem for him. Edward continued to be a happy baby. Brett however, was not a happy person and was unpleasant to be around.

We had been having some serious discussions about the same old stuff. We were always arguing about money: about buying formula, diapers, baby food, and baby clothes versus buying cigarettes and gambling on horses. Brett's first priority was not his family. But he didn't hit me or kick me again during our heated discussions.

My body took about three weeks to heal after giving birth. Sex was comfortable, and I used a diaphragm for birth control. I didn't worry about too much about getting pregnant, though, because our love life was predictable.

But after New Year's, 1990, Brett lost all interest in sex with me. We continued to argue about money and priorities.

In January, the therapist I was seeing for about seven years, Jason, took another position within the hospital. I was assigned a new therapist, an older woman whom I saw on and off. Sometimes I brought Edward with me, and sometimes I didn't. She came right out and said she was a mandated reporter, and she would report me if she suspected child abuse.

I guess there was no easy way for someone to come right out and say that without it sounding like an insult. But how she said it came across as rude; there was really no easy way to say it. She was just doing her job.

A week or so later, I called my mother to complain about Brett; she agreed that I should leave him. I had a couple different jobs between January and March, and I sent Mom some money to hold for me. I made an appointment to see a counselor at the women's residence where I lived as a single teenager and eventually worked. The interview went well; I applied for welfare and picked a date to move. At home, Brett was getting more and more difficult to live with, and I was feeling like I wanted to move out sooner than planned.

I decided to leave peacefully on a Wednesday. Instead of Brett asking me to stay and wanting to work things out, he was happy with me leaving but didn't want me to take Edward. After I told Brett we were leaving, he started to be verbally abusive and said he should keep Edward so I could "find myself." I decided to call my mom and tell her how he was harassing and fighting with me.

My mother came over to talk to both of us. Brett told my Mom, "She's young and needs to find herself. She tries to do so much work and keeps trying to go to school—leave the baby with me. I'll take care of him."

"No way," I responded. "You have no routine. You're up until 2:00 AM and then sleep until 2:00 PM. You smoke two to three cartons of cigarettes a week. You don't do any cleaning. You don't cook for yourself—you don't even know how to take care of yourself, let alone a ten-month-old. I'm taking Edward with me."

Mom told Brett he had a lot of nerve to put his needs before the baby's. She told him his financial priorities were backward. The baby would not be safe with him, because he had no routine and no common sense. He wouldn't have supervised Edward properly.

"You don't have a job. You don't support Emily and Edward, and she needs to get out of here and give this baby a life," Mom said.

The conversation went back and forth for a few minutes, but Brett didn't argue any more after my mother kept coming back with answers as to why the baby was better off with me, not him. Brett stopped arguing.

After Mom's visit, I wanted to leave Brett as soon as possible, but I was uncomfortable leaving while he was home. On a Tuesday night, when Brett was bowling in a league, I called an emergency shelter to see if I could stay there for a few nights until I would be able to move to the women's residence. They had a room, but I had to find my own transportation there. I decided to take the bus; there was an 8:15 PM line-up downtown. We lived three blocks away from the bus stop.

I left too late, and as I was walking down the street with Edward in one arm and a suitcase, purse, and baby bag in the other arm, the bus whizzed by. I returned to the house and called the shelter again. The shelter couldn't pick me up, but I could still go if I needed to. The next bus line-up was downtown at 9:30 PM. This time, I was going to leave early enough to catch the bus. Brett still wouldn't be home yet.

It was mid-March and bitter cold outside. It was about twenty degrees, but the wind chill made it feel more like the single digits. It was very dark out. I left the house early this time so I wouldn't miss the bus again. On my way, a car pulled over, stopped, and rolled down the passenger's side window. An older woman with blond hair wrapped in a bun said, "Where are you going with that baby at this hour of the night?"

I replied, "I'm leaving my husband, and I'm catching the bus downtown to go to an emergency shelter."

"Do you want a ride?" she asked.

"Yes. Thank you. That would be great." I got in the car with Edward and all of our stuff, and I gave the woman directions to the shelter.

On the way, I told the woman about Brett's gambling and that I was taking this time to start over. She drove me all the way to the shelter and was very nice about it. Before I got out of the car, she gave me $30 and said, "Don't share this with your husband."

I replied, "Thank you very much, and I won't give any of it to my husband." I got out of the car, went to the shelter's back door, and rang the bell. Someone answered and let me in. I turned to the parking lot and waved to the woman in the car.

The shelter staff showed me to a room with a bed and portable crib. I left my stuff in the room, changed Edward's diaper, and returned to the office. I sat down with the staff person to fill out some paperwork and answer some questions.

The person who did the paperwork was not friendly. She seemed to be an unhappy person, and she didn't seem to be supportive with my decision to leave my husband. I was anxious enough as it was because Brett didn't know I had left. I asked to use the phone so I could leave a message on my mom's answering machine. I wanted her to know I left Brett a few days early. I had no income because I took a temporary leave of absence from my job.

I was able to get Brett to buy two bags of diapers on the first of each month and give me $50 in cash. We were cordial for the next two months, and he helped me with rides to Edward's doctor's appointments and grocery shopping.

Edward was tall for his age at eleven months old. His weight was very good, and he was babbling and saying some words. His first phrase was "Hi baby." He was still a happy baby. I was okay, too, and I was looking forward to the nicer weather. I wanted to get out more.

I was invited back to Buffalo to see Miss Clara, the staff person from the residential school. We had kept in touch ever since I left: we talked on the phone, wrote letters or postcards back and forth, and she had invited me to stay at her house for a few days with Edward. We were celebrating his first birthday. I was going to get a bus ticket, but my mother supplemented the cost and insisted that we take the train.

Edward and I visited Clara, her husband, and their daughter for about four days. She had a playpen that we used for Edward at naptime and bedtime. We had a small pre-birthday party for Edward, and Clara videotaped it for us. During the four days that we were there, we did a lot of talking, baked cookies, had the small birthday party, went to the mall, and Clara even bought me an outfit. It was a nice break away from home.

When I returned home, Mom picked me up at the train station. We talked about a birthday party for Edward. We planned the party for Saturday, May 26; it would be on the back patio of the women's residence.

My parents hadn't seen each other for about five years, since my high school graduation. They didn't talk at all during this time, because there was no need. But I invited my mother, father, his wife, and my grandmother Washborne to Edward's birthday party.

My grandmother was fussy about the cake. She demanded that she buy it from a bakery, and then she rubbed the cost of the cake in my face. But it was delicious.

I decorated the patio with balloons, and I bought soda and chips and took pictures. It was a nice party. Edward had a big smile on his face while he was eating his cake, and he was laughing and clapping his hands during the party. He received many gifts for his first birthday, and we all had a good time.

Chapter 15

Remember Me?

In June 1990, my mother and I decided to live together. Mom found a luxurious two-bedroom apartment across from the community college. Edward and I shared the larger of the two bedrooms, and Mom took the smaller one. It was a beautiful and safe place to live; the only problem was that it was not on a decent bus line.

I was twenty-five years old, and I didn't have a driver's license or a learner's permit. I didn't even know how to pump gas. I had never been encouraged to learn to drive, so I used the city's bus system instead. But the city bus only came by the apartment complex four times a day and not at all on Sundays. This made me more dependent on Mom for transportation.

I decided to try college once again (I had enrolled in business school about a year prior, but Brett was less than thrilled about me being a student at the time), and I went to the community college across from where my mother and I were living. I signed up for four courses and managed to get free daycare for Edward. I was on welfare at the time, and this was my big opportunity to get an education and better myself. I always wanted to be a teacher; I hoped to obtain a two-year degree from the college to reach part of this goal, and then maybe continue on to a four-year school.

I flirted with Brett to give him the impression that we could try again, and he rejected me several times. I wanted to be in a relationship with someone, because I didn't feel complete without a man. I hoped John, the neighbor I had a few years back, was still single; I looked up his number in the phone book and was very excited to see that it was listed.

"Hello?" John answered.

"Hi, John. It's me, Emily from Seneca Street. Remember me?"

"Yes, How's it going?"

"Good," I said. Then, after a brief pause, "Are you still single?"

"Yup. And you?"

"I am. I left my husband in March, and it looks like it's over. I have my son Edward, and we live in a women's residence in an old building on the Children's Center Campus."

"Oh, okay. How old is Edward?"

"He's almost one. He's a good baby."

"That's great. I'm glad you called."

"Me too," I replied. Then, after working up a bit of courage, I added, "Do you want to get together sometime?"

"Sure. How about dinner on Tuesday?"

"Yeah, I would like that. How about 5:30 PM at Friendly's?"

"I like Friendly's; I'll pick you up at 5:30 PM."

"Okay, see you then. Bye bye."

"Alright, Emily. See you and Edward then. Bye for now."

John and I ended up seeing each other on the weekends, and Edward was getting used to being around him. John, like Peter, didn't take well to casual sex. We had a traditional courtship, once again, for a few months.

In December, I took the written test to get my learner's permit. I was in the car a lot with John—he was a nervous driver—and his driving inspired me to take my permit test. It was about time I learned how to drive. And it would help me out a lot, since I lived so far from the bus line.

I had to order my birth certificate from Iowa in order to complete the paperwork for my learner's permit, and it took about a week to arrive.

I was a little nervous and my hands were sweating the day I sat down at the DMV to take the test. It took about thirty minutes before I was called in to the exam room. I took my seat and the test administrator handed me my test.

There were twenty questions on the sheet, mostly about alcohol consumption. After I finished my test, I took it up to the test administrator, and she corrected it right in front of me. My heart was pounding—there was that ticking clock in my chest again. You were only allowed to miss four questions in order to pass the test, and I missed three. I was so happy; this was a great move toward my independence.

I stayed at the community college for one semester but ended up dropping two of the four courses. I was very insecure and unmotivated. In addition, I was depressed and didn't really do anything for my depression. I didn't like my replacement therapist, so I was discharged from the Hamilton Psychiatric Hospital. I had a visit with the clinic's psychiatrist, and he agreed that because I was a parent, maybe Child and Family Services would be a better place for me to receive counseling. I was no longer an outpatient psychiatric patient.

I stayed in English 099, which was a non-credit course. I passed the course, and if I decided to return, I would be eligible to take the first for-credit English course offered. The other course I kept was in career counseling. The teacher was really boring. I did a lot of writing assignments for the class. I loved to write, so I completed most of the assignments, but my attendance was not all that great. I got a "C" in the course.

In January, I decided to return to business school. The business school was small, on a better bus line, and I just couldn't handle regular college. To me, the courses at the business school were a little easier. The community college was a big school, and because I didn't seek help for anything, it just seemed harder. In retrospect, I should have looked into taking college preparation courses at the downtown Educational Opportunity Center before trying college at the business school or community college.

By June, I had filed for a divorce from Brett. I chose to go through the free lawyer service downtown. The paperwork really shouldn't have taken that long, because it was a simple divorce without property to divide, but because it was free, they could take their time finishing the paperwork and submitting it to the judge.

John and I went to visit a pastor of the church I had attended with Brett. Brett was part of the church's softball team, but he usually didn't attend services. John and I joined the church and started attending, and then we made an appointment to see the pastor to ask him to marry us. Since I was not yet divorced, the pastor couldn't marry John and me, so we made a very thoughtless and selfish decision: we decided to get pregnant.

John had a minimum wage job with no health insurance, and we didn't live together. I was not working and already had one child. If I brought another baby into our life, what would that do to the attention Edward needed from me? And what would this do to us financially?

We weren't thinking about anyone but ourselves; we were rushing. Our relationship had just started again eight months prior, I was not divorced yet, and we didn't have money.

I decided not to tell my mother right away, because I knew she would be very angry. I was saving up my money to get an apartment in Hamilton. I needed to be on my own with Edward—I didn't want to be talked into an abortion or adoption—and I also didn't like living so far outside of the city without decent transportation. I didn't think Mom would be supportive when she found out I was pregnant again.

I loved my mother, and I was grateful to her for helping me move out of the women's residence. I was also grateful for the time

I had with her. At that point, she had been diagnosed with cancer again.

She wanted Edward and me to have a nice place to live, and I was a big help to her, sharing expenses and some of the chores. She had also taken great care to make sure Edward had everything he needed.

I found a small one-bedroom apartment I could afford on the north side of Hamilton, and Edward and I moved in April. Before making the move, I told my mother I was pregnant.

Mom was cleaning the kitchen. She always believed in doing a thorough job. She was wiping down the counters, and right before she started the dishwasher, I asked her if I could talk to her so the noise wouldn't be distracting. She stopped what she was doing and sat at the dining room table. Edward was in the playpen.

"Mom, I have something to tell you."

"What is it?" she asked, as if she knew it may not be good news.

"I'm pregnant."

"*What?* Are you kidding me? What is wrong with you?" she screamed, backing away from the table.

I tried to worm my way out by saying I missed a pill, which was not the truth. I very willingly stopped taking the pill. It was an excellent method of birth control for me.

"It's true. That is why we are moving out."

"You'll go crazy with two kids, and foster care with take them and adopt them out," she said all in one breath. She got up from the table and went into the kitchen to turn the dishwasher on. Our conversation was over.

I didn't know where I was going to get prenatal care now that my mom was so angry with me. She still worked at the hospital where I gave birth to Edward, and I wasn't sure if I wanted to be at her hospital or not. John worked at the other hospital in the area, and I was thinking I should have the baby at his hospital.

Edward and I were still getting settled in to our tiny apartment. I had a counseling session with a Purchase Preventive worker for about forty-five minutes; she took the place of the therapist I had at the psychiatric hospital.

The worker came to the house twice a month to see me for counseling and coaching with independent living skills. But, in order to qualify for a Purchase Preventive worker, that worker would have to submit paperwork to the children's division department that described reasons the child was at risk for placement in foster care, if this service was not provided.

I was depressed and unfocused. One of my goals in my work with the Purchase Preventative worker may have been to follow a strict routine with Edward, especially making sure he gets breakfast, lunch, and dinner. Another goal may have been to stay on top of his doctor's appointments. Edward was one year old and would need shots at one year, fifteen months, and eighteen months old.

I didn't have a lot of support or many friends, and I ended up looking to workers as if they were my friends.

I went to a family center that had an evening respite for parents who were in crisis. Sometimes I took a taxi there, which the program paid for. Once, Edward and I were waiting for a bus to go to the family center. Edward got away from me, and started running toward the street. I instinctively grabbed him by his hair, not maliciously, but just because that was the part of him closest to my fingertips, and because I didn't want him to be hit by a bus. He was two years old and very active. I did it to save his life, not to physically hurt him. I went to the family center and opened my big mouth about what had happened.

Shortly after doing so, I had a counseling session with my PPS worker. As the PPS worker was leaving, another social worker showed up from Child Protective Services. He had a report of suspected child abuse, neglect, or mal-treatment. The PPS worker decided to go back upstairs to my apartment and hear the charges against me. Someone reported that I pulled Edward's hair, didn't give him enough playtime between dinner and bedtime, and I was rough with his arms. My heart was pounding so fast. I couldn't believe someone would think I abused Edward by pulling him from any body part I could to stop him from being hit by a bus.

The playtime between dinner and bedtime was silly because we lived across the street from a playground and went over almost every single night. Edward would run around and play for at least a half hour before we went into the apartment for the night. The worker wrote down some notes and talked to Roxy, the PPS worker, and claimed he would get back to me.

The pregnancy was going well, except I was having morning sickness about two weeks longer than my first pregnancy. I was a little big for three and a half months, and my bladder was weaker for a longer period of time in the beginning. The family physician didn't suspect anything unusual, though.

At the end of May, I decided to have my prenatal care at the hospital where John worked. The doctor ordered a sonogram to confirm pregnancy time and delivery dates.

In the doctor's office, I got undressed, put a gown on, and waited for the sonogram technician to come in. Then I got on the table and lied down. The technician put the cold gooey stuff and then the transducer on my belly. He pulled the screen toward him and looked like he saw something. After a few minutes of reading his body language, I asked, "Is everything okay?"

"Yes ma'am. It looks here like you are having fraternal twins."

I started to giggle a little. He turned the screen toward me and pointed out the two heads separated by two sacs. At this time, he could not tell the sex of the twins.

I cried a little, but not too much, as he finished taking measurements of the two babies. He gave me several pictures and wished me all the best.

John would be out of work shortly, so I called his department and asked him to meet me in front of the hospital so I could show him the sonogram. I didn't say anything about the twins.

I sat on a bench in front of the hospital to wait. He met me about fifteen minutes later. It was a nice day out; the sun was shining with one or two clouds in the sky and a light breeze, which made for perfect weather.

"Hey, how's it going?" I asked.

"Good. What's up; everything okay?"

"Yes, but there is some news. Check this out," I said, showing John the sonogram and pointing to the two heads. "See? This is a head, and this is another head," I said with a coy smile. "We are having twins."

"What?"

"We are having fraternal twins! My due date is November 20. I see our family doctor next week for a follow-up."

"Oh my God! Wow," he said, putting his hand to his cheek and looking a little faint.

"So, well, I guess we should get married—you think?"

"Yes, Emily. Let's do it! I'll call the pastor tomorrow on one of my breaks, okay?"

"Yeah, I think we should try to keep the same date that we talked about with the pastor; it will give us enough time to plan and save some money."

"Sure, that sounds good to me!" he said, shaking his head in disbelief. "*Wow!* Twins. I can't believe it."

"Hey, I wanted twins, remember?"

"When Emily?"

"I used to talk about it all the time with my manager at McDonald's, Alice. I used to tell her all the time that I would just love to have a set of twins."

"Why?"

"Because my stepmom had Cindy and Susan; they wore the same outfits, they had each other to play with, and they were adorable."

"Oh, I see."

"Well, get your butt home and make some calls, and I will call you later. I have to pick up Edward from daycare and make some calls myself," I said, grinning ear to ear.

"Yes ma'am."

"You're funny. When I was younger, we would say, 'Ten-four, Sarge.'"

"Okay, ma'am; ten-four, ma'am."

"Get outta' here. Call me later; I gotta go."

"Okay, see you later or talk to you later or whatever"

John walked toward his car, still shaking his head. He even skipped a few steps like a little kid skipping with joy.

I caught the next city bus downtown to pick up Edward from daycare. I think I was more excited about having twins than getting married.

John worked hard for the next several months and saved money up for us to get married. We met with the pastor of the church whom we spoke with previously and attended three sessions of premarital counseling. I thought the best way to answer the pastor's questions was to say what I thought he wanted to hear, instead of speaking the truth.

My second wedding was to be in a church, before God. There was no backing out for me; we would have to live with our differences. I really didn't think too much about the actual wedding, because John did all the planning. I was concerned primarily about Edward and the care of our newborn twins.

John was very insecure and indecisive about a lot of things. He was not a strong person; he was weak, forgetful, insensitive, a smoker, and a drinker. I didn't know how he would overcome his weakness, insensitivity, and lack of decision-making, but he had promised to quit smoking, and I knew for sure he would quit drinking because we were together all the time.

He agreed that while the children were in the house, there would be no alcohol. I was a little surprised that he was a drinker because of what he went through growing up. His stepfather, George, was a heavy beer drinker, and his mother became one, too.

George and Betty's main focus was always beer, cigarettes, and food. George never laid a hand on John, his brother, or sisters, but he over-punished them for small misgivings. John and his siblings spent an unreasonable amount of time in their bedrooms on punishment.

George didn't make a lot of money, and he was out of work around Christmastime almost every year. The family struggled financially throughout John's childhood, and George didn't quit drinking until after John moved out of the house. Within a few months of quitting, George was diagnosed with cancer. He died about two years later.

My mother's mother was also an alcoholic, and she was physically violent and verbally abusive toward anyone who was around when she was drunk: my mother and my uncle when they were children, and she had a physical altercation with my mother in front of me once, when I was about eleven.

I hated her behavior when she was binging on her beloved vodka. She was 100 percent Irish and 100 percent miserable most of the time. I didn't want to be like her. I promised myself I would never drink like she did. I also promised myself that when I had children, I would not drink in front of them or expose them to that lifestyle.

The pregnancy was going well, but I didn't know anything about how to have a wedding. My first wedding was by a justice of the peace. We went out to dinner afterward, and that was it. I didn't know anything about planning the bridal shower, arranging for flowers, music—and I really didn't care. John wanted to make plans because he thought he knew more about weddings.

We started out with John's brother, Jeff, and sister-in-law, Mary, for the best man and matron of honor. At the bridal shower—that I didn't want—I got into an argument with Mary. We changed the matron of honor and best man to John's sister, Laura, and best friend, Paul.

If I really thought in my heart that John should be my husband, I should've planned a nice wedding when we were ready, instead of getting pregnant first. But, because I put myself in this situation, I didn't want a bridal shower, because I didn't feel worthy to celebrate.

Bridal showers should include a mother and future mother-in-law, sexy lingerie, maybe a dirty male dancer, and it should be a time for *lots* of fun. But here I was, five and a half months pregnant during a hot summer. I was uncomfortable and made the choice not to drink alcohol, so having a bridal shower was just not going to be much fun.

We were married on August 31, 1991. It was a very hot and humid day. The ceremony was scheduled for 11:00 AM. Everyone who was invited showed up, and it was a nice ceremony. Afterward, almost everyone went downstairs into the fellowship hall for chips, soda, and the cutting of the cake.

We had planned on a second reception at a local restaurant where John's two sisters worked. It was a buffet-style restaurant, which had large rooms that could be reserved for free. My father and stepmother didn't stay for this part of the evening but Grandmother Washborne did.

John's sister Laura agreed to keep Edward while we went to Niagara Falls, New York for a short honeymoon. Before we went, John packed up sandwiches and iced tea for snacks on the way so we wouldn't waste money on the thruway rest stops. We stopped once overnight before getting to Canada and arrived early Sunday morning. The traffic was very heavy.

John and I moved in together to a small two-bedroom apartment on the north side of the city before the wedding. Our neighbors were not shy about drinking and being a little rowdy. When the time came closer to having the twins, we decided to move again.

We moved further north of the city, in older Hamilton. John's sister and brother-in-law lived next door. We got along well, and she had a daughter who was about eighteen months old. John's sister, Terry, was willing to help me with Edward.

I went to all of my pre-natal appointments after the wedding. My family physician was a resident at the hospital's family practice, and this was his first time he would be delivering a set of twins. I was considered a high risk because I was having twins.

One of the sonograms showed the sex of the babies: a boy and girl.

Chapter 16

Double Duty

On November 11, 1991, I woke up suddenly at 5:00 AM to the sharp pang of cramps. Thinking they were contractions, I called the hospital after an hour, and the nurse told me to come right away. John got my bag and the twins' diaper bags, and we took Edward next door to his sister Terry's house.

I signed in to the admissions department at 6:30 AM and then went up to Labor and Delivery. I changed into a gown, and the nurse hooked me up to two monitors to keep track of the contractions and the babies' heartbeats.

The doctors and nurses referred to the twins as Baby A and Baby B. John and I had decided on the name Monica for our daughter and Patrick for our son.

After a few hours and a few phone calls by John, my mother came to the hospital to see me.

Around 11:00 AM, my labor started to slow down, and I didn't have any more contractions. But the babies' heartbeats were fine, and they were doing well. A couple hours later, my uterus stopped contracting, and the hospital sent me home. I was very disappointed. The sonogram had shown the estimated weights of each twin to be at least six pounds or more. The first baby was in a frank breech position.

Mom and John were with me, and as we were leaving the hospital, we saw our family physician.

"Next time I go into labor, I'm going to Saint Helen's," I said to him in a child-like voice.

"Don't do that," he warned. "They will section you."

At the end of the week, I had another sonogram that showed Baby A in the birth canal, still in a breech position. Baby B was in a transverse position—sideways.

I saw the obstetrician a few days later, and it was decided I should have a cesarean section. The doctor's office scheduled the surgery for the next day, November 19. I would go back to the hospital later that day to spend the night.

When I got home, I decided to eat a sandwich because I knew it might be my last decent meal for a few days. The cesarean was major surgery, and I had to fast from midnight that night until the following morning. I love to eat, and I was eating for three. I also tinkered around the house a little bit before going to the hospital.

I signed in to admissions at 2:00 PM (an hour late) and gave all my information to the admissions clerk. She offered me a wheelchair to go up to the maternity ward, but I wanted to walk.

When the admissions clerk and I were standing at the elevators, I felt a gushing from below my waist. Suddenly, my legs were wet.

"I've changed my mind; I'd like a wheelchair, please."

The admission clerk got a wheelchair, and I was taken up to the maternity ward. I got into my room, and the first thing I did was to go to the bathroom. When I wiped myself, there was a green-colored discharge on the toilet paper.

I pressed the button to get the nurse to come in my room. "Yes, do you need something?" a scratchy voice asked over the intercom.

"Hi, can someone come in here, please? I have a problem."

Nurse Bonnie walked into the room. "How can I help you?"

"Hi. Um . . . look, there's green on this toilet paper."

The nurse said she would be right back, and when she returned, she brought something to test the green discharge.

The test showed the first baby had moved her bowels. The next thing I knew, several people were in the room asking me all sorts of questions. While being heavily interrogated, I started to have contractions. I called my mother, the family physician's office, and John.

John was working in the hospital at the time, and he made a beeline for the maternity floor. Soon, I started to have more intense and painful contractions. The nurse had me hooked me up to two fetal monitors. She put this jelly-gooey stuff on my belly, and then she attached two belts with two small black boxes to my stomach. This allowed the nurses and doctors to hear both babies' heartbeats and measure the contractions.

When the nurse and doctors came in to check on me after a little while, and I was still in pain with contractions, I became frustrated by the same questions being asked over and over.

I said, "Aren't the answers to your questions in my chart somewhere? I've been coming here for seven months—where are the records?" I refused to answer any more questions.

One doctor came in, knowing I had a scheduled cesarean, and asked me, "Emily, do you really want a cesarean?"

I didn't realize that by pushing out the twins naturally, the recovery would be so much easier. My answer was, "Yes, I do."

The doctor ordered a catheter to be inserted, and shortly after a nurse followed his orders, he left the room. He didn't bother to check my cervix to see how much more I had dilated before leaving. Just then, our family physician came into the room to see me and said, "Hi, Emily. How's it going?"

I responded with heavy grunts and a pinched face; the contractions were getting closer together. "I think I'm having the twins very soon," I finally said. Our family doctor did a cervix check, and I was measuring at seven centimeters dilated. He was pissed off at the medical staff for not paying closer attention and checking me sooner.

I felt the urge to push. The doctor and nurses stood near me, held my legs back, and urged me to push with all my might. It was now time to get a stretcher and go to the delivery room. One of the nurses told John, who had a coffee in his hand, "Get your scrubs on! We're going to Labor and Delivery."

I moved to the stretcher, and Nurse Bonnie was still nearby. She was beautiful, with thick blond hair in a Farrah Fawcett hairstyle. She was doing a great job coaching me through the painful contractions. "Don't push, Emily. Hold on and breathe. Breathe!" I blew out so hard that it looked like a fan was blowing her hair back. "Yes, do that Emily! Breathe. Breathe. Don't push, not yet. We're almost there," she continued.

As I was rushed to Labor and Delivery on a stretcher, with the doctor and nurses running alongside me, I was reminded me of scenes I'd seen in movies and on hospital shows on television. These folks were doing the same thing. I could almost hear the theme song from *The Young and the Restless*. For some reason, the Labor and Delivery floor of the hospital was nowhere near the maternity ward.

It was about 5:35 PM when I was brought into Labor and Delivery. The obstetrician on call had never met me before. He knew nothing about my situation. Our family physician and the on-call doctor got ready to deliver the first twin. The on-call doctor was told that the first twin had moved her bowels and was in the frank breech position.

"Of course she's going to take a shit—she's a full-term frank breech," he responded.

My legs were up on the stirrups, and I was more ready than ever to deliver the first twin. Monica was born before I could blink. She weighed seven pounds and seven and a half ounces. She had good lungs; her cry was loud. However, due to her bowels being moved, they had to have her in the neonatal nursery for at least four hours to watch her.

It was time for the next twin, who collapsed in my uterus after the first twin was born. The doctor decided to give me anesthesia to knock me out to deliver this second twin.

I didn't understand what was going on. They put a mask over my mouth to put me under, but didn't give me any directions to relax and count backward. So, I fought with my arms swinging around because I felt like they were cutting off my breathing. They instructed John to come to the head of the bed and hold my arms down. I was fighting John, and then decided on my own to relax and started counting to myself—*ten, nine, eight*—and I was out.

The on-call doctor decided to reach up into my uterus and deliver the second twin by pulling him out by his feet. Eight minutes later, at 5:54 PM, Patrick was born. He weighed eight pounds. My son was okay, alive, and had all his fingers and toes.

After the delivery of both babies, I was taken to recovery. The recovery nurse brought me a pan of water and handed me a washcloth. I had just delivered fifteen pounds and seven and a half ounces of combined weight, and I didn't feel like washing up. After about three hours of recovery, I returned to the maternity ward.

Monica was doing well in the special care nursery, and they brought her to me. But after a day, Patrick's sugar level was very low, and he was having a hard time eating. He went to the special care nursery. I took both babies at the same time and nursed them together and sometimes separately. Patrick really took a long time to eat.

On November 18, 1991, life had begun with our new family. I was very fortunate to have a very kind family physician who arranged for me to have a home health aide for the first two weeks of the twin's life. He also managed to give me an extra day in the hospital because I was breastfeeding the twins.

The attending obstetrician didn't see me after he delivered the twins. I only remember him cursing in the delivery room and delivering my second twin feet first. I believed in my heart, in the pit of my soul, that the delivery of Patrick by his feet may have caused him some brain damage, but there was no way to know until he was older.

Chapter 17

Getting into Everything

After we received our tax refund in February 1992, John and I decided to move to a bigger place. We were lucky to find a spacious and inexpensive three-bedroom upstairs apartment; the only bad aspects were that it was on a very busy street and had no backyard, but we made the most of it anyway.

Patrick was a happy and sweet baby; he was a good sleeper and was easy to please. But I noticed he was a little slow in his development; he was about one or two months behind Monica.

When the twins were six months old, I was working again as a home health aide and ended up with a client who was a child. He did some of the same things that Patrick did and would hold his bottle the same way. I was able to point out some of the similarities to our family physician during an appointment that fall.

I also mentioned that Patrick was still very slow at eating. He hadn't had normal bowel movements since he was born; he was on baby food and some finger foods, and he still got diarrhea. His arms and legs were stiff, he crawled with one arm and one leg, and at ten months, he wasn't close to being able to walk, not even while holding on to furniture. Our family physician wrote a letter to a neurologist to have Patrick evaluated.

After the evaluation, Patrick was labeled with a "non-specific neurological disorder." A teacher from an early childhood special education program started to come by the house weekly, and he also received weekly speech, occupational, and physical therapy.

That summer, my PPS worker and her coworkers created a support group for women who had suffered some sort of sexual abuse in their life. I had looked into groups like this before, but I seemed to always find incest groups, not groups for all types of sexual abuse.

The four PPS workers got five of us together once a week and we talked about our current issues, as well as the abuse we suffered in the past.

One of the women, Peggy, was expecting her ninth child. She had children from two years old to thirteen years old: four boys and four girls and another on the way. At the moment, she had custody of three of her children while the others had been placed in foster care. I complained in the group that I didn't have decent childcare to go grocery shopping or to go to the movies with John if we wanted. Peggy offered to babysit my children and said not to worry about the money.

I had been attending the women's support group every week. One week, Jennifer, a worker who provided childcare during the meetings, threatened to call Child Protective Services on me because Monica had a diaper rash.

I was a very cooperative client and parent. If someone made a suggestion, I didn't waste time before jumping up to do what he or she said. If I had a friend whose daughter was suffering from a diaper rash, I would ask them what they were doing. I would ask them if they had a prescription cream and suggest they may want to think about switching diaper brands. I certainly wouldn't threaten them with CPS.

The very next day, I made an appointment with the pediatrician for Monica to be seen for the rash. The physician sent me home with a prescription for cream, and I also got a note from the doctor, which I immediately took to Jennifer. I included the prescription package and an extra note specifically for her, letting her know that I take care of my children and that her threats were totally uncalled for.

After the incident, I didn't return to the group. I kept in touch with Peggy—who had left the group after her baby was born—by phone about once a week.

We lived on a hill, in a very busy area with lots of cars around. That winter, a neighbor caught sight of Edward and Monica sledding down the hill, unsupervised, without coats. Edward was three years old, and Monica was one.

I was in my bedroom at the time, folding laundry while I assumed the kids were still watching TV. The neighbor knocked on my door and brought Edward and Monica to me. were having the time of their life.

I made a phone call to tell my PPS worker, Roxy, to let her know what had happened. She wasn't in the office at the time, and there was no voicemail available.

Patrick's visiting nurse came to see him the day after the sledding incident. I described the situation to her about the kids being outside with no coats on, unsupervised, sledding together down the hill. I don't recall her asking me what I did to make the apartment and the kids safe so it never happened again. I don't remember her commenting about how lucky we all were that nothing bad had happened to the kids while they were outside, unsupervised. Instead, she called my PPS worker, who said she didn't know anything about it. My PPS worker said, "You heard it straight from her; go ahead and hotline her."

About two days later, the phone rang. It was a Child Protective Services worker with a thick German accent. She was very polite and said she needed to see me because a report had been made against me. She came over the next day. The apartment was clean and there was food in the fridge, but I was a little anxious and upset.

It was a big advantage for me that the assigned CPS worker didn't get along with my PPS worker. They seemed to have had some problems prior to this report. The CPS worker labeled the report "unfounded." This was a great relief for me because I didn't have to go to court, and I didn't have anything on my permanent record.

I gave Peggy a call soon after, and we started hanging out. I watched her youngest daughter for a few hours every Wednesday while she took her boys to counseling. I didn't charge her any money, because later in the week and sometimes on the weekend, she kept our three children while we cleaned the house, went shopping, or went to the movies.

Peggy's younger children were near the same age as Edward and Monica, and she recently had one of her older daughters, Ellen, come home from foster care. Ellen was eleven; she went to school and helped with the younger children. Sometimes she would come over to our house and watch our kids.

Children's Division had set up some classes and programs for Peggy to complete to get her other children out of foster care. She had a PPS worker, a parent aide, the boys went to counseling, and she had attended the sexual abuse group once a week. Peggy was very cooperative with everything she was required to do to get her kids back.

Peggy had a lot of workers in her life. She had an alliance worker—someone who would organize progress meetings with Peggy and all the workers on her case—and a parent aid who coached her on discipline and routine for the kids she had at home. She also had a PPS worker, a miserable person who didn't like anything about her job.

Sometimes when I was hanging out at Peggy's, if one of her children did something to irritate her, her reaction shocked me. When Paula, who was three, and Jason, who was two, were running around the house and would bump into the coffee table, knocking over her coffee, Peggy would yell out, "What the f***, man?" I was really surprised at her choice of words. Other times, she called her children names like "bastard," "slut," "whore," "f****' b****," etc.

In the beginning, I wondered if I should be hanging around her. I didn't talk like that, and I never really hung out with people who talked like that. But I was so desperate for a friend and someone to keep my kids for a few hours that I tuned her bad language out and pretended not to hear it. Her children would sometimes use bad words or phrases like "s*** my d***," "you c***sucker," "b***," etc. But Peggy talked like this and didn't think much about her kids cursing. Once, I asked her about her children swearing, and her response was, "They could be doing much worse than cussing."

Peggy's oldest daughter, Sandra, was currently at a residential facility, close to where they lived. She would make home visits, and the worker's in Peggy's life had told Sandra she could return home after a year. Well, one year had passed, and Peggy was still going to groups, had finished parenting classes, was always home for the parent aide, and saw the PPS worker like she was supposed to, but the courts were not letting Sandra come home. In return, Sandra rebelled and started to run away.

After a summer of running away, one of Peggy's sisters became a kinship foster parent to Sandra. Before she went to live with her aunt, Sandra got pregnant at fifteen years old. Shortly after she moved into her aunt's house, she ended up returning home because the aunt was not prepared to deal with a newborn baby. The one thing that got Sandra home with her mother, unfortunately, was getting pregnant.

Peggy was assigned a new foster care worker, Josephine, a very serious-looking older woman. Her objective was to get Peggy all of her children back. Within the next year, Derrick and Annie came home. She then had Sandra, fifteen; Ellen, twelve; Annie, nine; Derrick, seven; Paula, four; Jason, three; and Katelynn, one.

Patrick was being evaluated for his developmental delay, and I also had Edward evaluated because he was doing some strange things. Unfortunately, when I was interviewed for Edward, I gave a lot of information about my childhood and adolescent life and about Edward's biological father.

Instead of someone suggesting the Head Start preschool program for Edward, he was labeled "emotionally disturbed"—in my opinion, based more on his parent's history—and he was assigned to a special education preschool for three-year-olds. Peggy warned me about giving too much information, but I didn't listen.

It was almost the summer of 1993; the twins were nineteen months old, and Edward had just turned four. We still lived in a two-bedroom basement apartment of the complex in Dewitt, a small suburb outside of Hamilton, where John worked. It was not easy having three kids in one bedroom. The kids were getting older, and we were thinking about finding a bigger place.

John decided to give notice and move us back to Hamilton, where he was able to find a job for a real estate company. But it was not the best job for him, and after two weeks, he realized it was not working out. Before he left this job, we moved to another second floor apartment on the inner city's north side. We didn't realize how bad the area was until it was too late.

The landlord found a tenant for the downstairs apartment—a wild drug and alcohol user. He was a single man who partied every night, all night. We suspected he sold drugs, too, because a lot of people came in and out of his apartment all day and all night. Somebody threw a brick through his window once.

We were visiting Peggy one evening, and Monica, who was two years old and quite a klutz, fell and hit her face against a footstool in the living room. She got two black eyes. I knew her face would heal, and when she went to daycare, I told the staff what had happened. It didn't appear to be a problem until about a month later.

In early October 1993, I needed to go shopping, so John was going to stay home with the kids. John was usually very tired after work but made a sincere effort to keep the kids as safe as possible. This one particular day, John was in Edward's bedroom and moved the dresser in front of the door so all three kids would be in the room with him. He figured he could rest and the kids would stay safe. While John was resting, Edward took the shoelaces out of his sneakers and put the strings around his neck, leaving a red mark behind.

The next day, I went to the daycare and told the truth about what had happened. Patrick also had a lump on his wrist. The staff pointed it out to me, and I had Patrick at the pediatrician's office within twenty-four hours. He had an x-ray, which showed it was a lymph node infection. There were no signs of this infection except for the lump. I hadn't noticed it, but as soon as someone pointed it out to me, I was at the doctor's office.

Unfortunately, the director of the daycare center decided to hotline me over Monica's two black eyes, Patrick's lump on his wrist (the report said it got caught in the bars on his crib, although he didn't sleep in a crib at that time) and the marks on Edward's neck. Two state workers visited the daycare center as a result. They had the kids take their clothes off and took photos of their injuries. Then the two workers came to see me.

Edward's father, Brett, was not doing well. From the first day I met Brett, he had taken three pills at night, religiously. But Brett had decided to stop taking his medication that summer. He thought he didn't need to take it anymore.

Brett's mother, Lucy, moved back to her first floor apartment from the adult home she had been living in. Brett was now "taking care" of his mother, although he didn't get Lucy her medication and did not have her attend her day program at the Hamilton Psychiatric Hospital. He basically took her Social Security and veteran's check, leaving Lucy home alone, and gambled at the horse track. Her health was suffering because of his neglect.

We decided to move out of our apartment because our neighborhood was loud and filled with drugs, and our downstairs neighbor constantly had parties and people coming in and out of the house. On one of our last days in the bad neighborhood, a check came in the mail addressed to Brett Kendall. Out of curiosity, I opened the envelope and found a check for $29,990. I called Brett, who I had not been in touch with for about three months. When he came over, he looked terrible.

The last time Edward visited Brett and his mother, I was very uneasy about how Brett was acting, so I stopped the visits. I even made a call to Adult Protective Services because I thought Brett's mother, Lucy, was not being properly taken care of. She didn't appear clean to me, and I knew Brett was spending her Social Security and veteran's check on gambling and not on her medication. The APS worker came over to investigate but didn't see anything wrong at that time.

Brett came over to get the check, and I was shocked at his physical and mental condition. He was whispering under his breath, his eyes were filled with crust, and he looked like he had lost about forty pounds. I had never, in the eight years I had known him, seen him in such poor condition. I was very upset and very concerned as I handed him the check.

About an hour later, I put the kids in the car, took them over to my sister-in-law's, and went straight to Brett's house. I brought him to the bank and helped him deposit some of the money from the check into his savings account and take some cash out for himself. Then we went back to his house. His mother looked like she had been in the same clothes for weeks.

I made a phone call to the Adult Protective worker and explained the situation. I was totally annoyed with that department and with the worker who indicated there was not enough evidence to show that Lucy was not properly taken care of.

I took Brett to the county's central location for psychiatric evaluations. I was hoping they would recognize he'd had a psychotic episode and it was medically necessary for him to be hospitalized.

It was really obvious to me that Brett had gone off his medication, and his body couldn't handle the adjustment. I left him at the hospital, where he stayed overnight. It was with grave concern for Brett as a human being, not as my ex-husband, that I brought him there. The hospital made a terrible error in judgment and discharged Brett two days later, with paper prescriptions to fill.

I went back to Brett's house while he was still in the hospital to figure out what to do about his mother. I called some home care agencies to see if I could pay cash for an aide to come over and sit with her while Brett was in the hospital. I couldn't get anyone to come over.

I helped Lucy into the bathroom to assist her with washing up and changing her clothes. She was completely hunched over and having a very hard time just walking. It took her almost half an hour to get from the dining room table to the bathroom, six feet away. The underwear I found for her was very tight, but she wore it anyway.

I called an ambulance, and the emergency medical technician listened to Lucy's lungs and took her to the hospital based on the possibility of bronchitis.

Brett was let out the next day from the hospital. He had thousands in the bank and was anxious to spend it. He didn't fill his prescriptions and continued to suffer through the mental psychosis.

Brett was obsessed with Martians; he would walk outside and look up in the sky, convinced they were coming to Earth. Without a belt, Brett had lost so much weight that his pants would fall to the ground as he'd stare into the night sky. His neighbors witnessed this behavior.

For about six weeks, Brett continued to spend his money. He bought a new car, paid some bills, and went gambling. In the beginning of December, he was involved in a car accident, but left the scene of the crime. A police officer caught up with him at his house. It was obvious that Brett was sick and needed help. The police officer offered him a choice between jail or the hospital. Brett chose the hospital.

At this time, his condition grew significantly worse. Two physicians were smart enough to agree that Brett needed hospitalization. Poor Brett had to commit a crime in order to get help for his condition. He spent the next three months in the hospital.

I was devastated and lost all faith in the psychiatric system. They truly neglected Brett from the first visit I made with him when they turned him away with a paper prescription. This was all very emotionally painful for me because I knew Brett when he was healthy.

Brett's mother remained in the hospital. The suspected bronchitis was actually pneumonia, and she also had a severe hypothyroid condition. Adult Protective Services proceeded to take Brett to court and take away his payee rights to Lucy's Social Security and veteran's benefits.

Shortly after I saw to Brett and Lucy's problems, I began having some problems of my own. I missed a period and went to have a pregnancy test. The first one, a blood test, came out negative. The second one, a urine test taken at the clinic downtown, was positive. We were now going to have our fourth child.

Mom had moved to California the previous year to be closer to my sister who had moved out a few years earlier and recently had a baby. Mom wanted to be there and to start a new life with her. She sold almost all her belongings and went with the intention of getting a job and starting over. Connie was still pregnant, due the end of July, when Mom moved to California in early June 1992.

In early November, we moved again to another apartment complex where John's sister lived. We were neighbors again.

When we received our tax refunds in 1994, we decided to move to a wonderful four-bedroom apartment with one and a half baths. I was pregnant again and due in the beginning of June. Peggy's fifteen-year-old daughter, Sandra, and I were pregnant at the same time.

Chapter 18

Number Four

John was working at the mall, and I was pregnant with our fourth child. The twins were two and a half. Patrick had been tested for his developmental delays and was attending a preschool program for early childhood special education, and Monica was a typical two-year-old, not attending daycare or preschool. Edward went with Patrick to the same early childhood program for his diagnosis of emotionally disturbed.

I was taking some parenting classes at the family center, and I met a woman there, Bianca, whom I tried to be friends with. She was a heavyset girl like me, only shorter and a bit bigger. I offered to pick her up and drop her off from the class to save on gas. She had a daughter Edward's age, and I really needed a friend.

At the start of each parenting class, there was time set aside for drinking coffee and socializing. Bianca was very social and wanted to be there for this time, so she was frustrated with me when I was late picking her up a few times. As a result, she decided to hotline me to Child Protective Services.

The hotline report stated that I left the twins unsupervised in the house, which was not true. We explained what had happened to the CPS worker: I was late picking up Bianca for class one day, and since the twins were playing on the phone and my line was busy, she assumed no one was in the house.

Needless to say, I stopped going to the parenting program and was no longer friends with Bianca.

We were assigned a new PPS worker. I had requested a change; Roxy was a nice person, but she was too religious for me at the time. This new PPS worker was excellent at counseling John and I together. She labeled the report "unfounded."

I had prenatal appointments each week in June. The baby was doing well, but it seemed as though she was not ready to be born on her due date, which was right around the corner.

On a warm Thursday in June, I was feeling well enough to go to bingo at St. Patrick's, a church about four blocks away from where we lived. I was irritated with John, and we argued before he dropped me off. I played bingo for fun, even though in the back of my mind I was thinking about how I would spend the money if I won.

That evening, I won the coverall before the intermission—a whopping $250! I was the only winner, and I called John to tell him I was sorry for acting like I did and to let him know that I had won the coverall. He picked me up when bingo was over, and we spent the money on things for the new baby.

I went to the doctor's the following day for a sonogram. The technician told me I was low on fluid and the baby was in a breech position. A cesarean section was scheduled for the next day, Saturday, July 2. I went home, gathered everything I needed, and kissed and hugged the twins and Edward.

I was admitted to the ninth floor this time. My mother could not be there, but she was waiting patiently by the phone in California to hear that the baby was born and healthy.

Mom had arrived in California about a month before my sister's first baby was born. She began experiencing pain in her face and, assuming it was a sinus infection, she set up an appointment to get it checked out.

Instead of a sinus infection, the pain was caused by a tumor on each cheek—terminal cancer. My sister and I both hoped Mom would live until the end of January 1995, when Connie was expecting her second baby.

On Saturday, July 2, I was prepped for the cesarean and taken to Labor and Delivery. I was given a spinal tap to numb the lower half of my body for surgery. The baby was in a breech position, and I insisted on a cesarean because Patrick didn't do well during natural childbirth.

Since I would be opened up anyway, I thought this would be a great opportunity to get my tubes tied. Unfortunately, the midwife involved in my prenatal care went to the clinic to look for papers I had signed to have my tubes tied, but it appeared they had been misplaced.

John was with me at the hospital, and we had a babysitter for the three kids. I was awake for this surgery, but I didn't feel much. I felt a little tugging but nothing painful. It was 10:11 AM when Isabella was born. She was healthy and had all her fingers and toes. John held her first and made me feel good when he said, "She looks like you." I was okay, and after I was stapled and stitched back up, I went off to recovery.

I didn't like the pain I was feeling in my stomach. It was very uncomfortable, and I complained about it. I breastfed Isabella, and she was doing very well. She wasn't as big as the other three; she weighed a little more than seven pounds and was twenty inches long.

Isabella had a soft cry. I got up like I was supposed to and walked around to soothe her, but the pain in my stomach was awful. The nurses came in twice during every eight-hour shift to take my temperature, and at one point, it was slightly elevated. I had a fever a couple days after Isabella was born, and I was given triple antibiotics through an IV. After another day, my fever went higher. Finally, six days after I'd given birth, the doctors took me off the antibiotics, and my fever started to go down. Soon I was well enough to be discharged.

I was in the hospital the whole time John was on vacation from work, and my husband and the kids were ready for me to come home. The smile on John's face when he picked Isabella and I up from the hospital was priceless.

Mom was not doing well; her cancer started to spread throughout the rest of her body. I began to believe her time was coming soon. I started to think I wasn't going to get to see her again, and she would never meet Isabella.

I sent my mom photos and wrote her letters constantly. But I didn't hold back all my worries, frustrations, and problems; I was not thoughtful about her illness. I wrote her about things that were bothering me, not thinking that I was burdening her while she was suffering her own pain.

Mom passed away on a Sunday in September, and my sister called me the next day to tell me. I was very sad, but I was also at peace that my mother was no longer suffering. In the end, she had double vision and was in a lot of pain. She had just turned forty-eight.

John's mother Betty had been renting a house on the north side of the city for about ten years. After her husband had passed away from cancer and her five children were all grown, Betty applied for subsidized housing for herself. Her name came up on the list in August, and she moved in September. Her old house seemed big enough for the six of us, so we moved in about a week after Mom passed away.

My sister Connie came to Hamilton to bring some items my mother wanted me to have. Right up until Mom passed away, Connie always sent John, the kids, and I birthday and Christmas cards. She would ask about the kids with genuine interest. But in the pit of my soul, I knew once Mom died that Connie would cut me off forever. And she did.

I was only concerned with myself at the time; I was really selfish, greedy and ungrateful. Connie didn't know how to deal with me. I was not her responsibility, and we didn't have anything in common.

She went to college, she started a serious career, and then she had her children. She did everything the right way, and I did things backward.

Mom had her wishes about her life insurance policy clearly stated. She discussed it with me toward the end of her life several times. Connie lived in the same state as Mom, and, because she was more responsible than me, she was the executor of Mom's estate.

The money would be divided in half, after expenses. My four children and Connie's two children would each receive savings bonds for their education. This money would stay in a trust until they were of age to use it for higher education or until they were twenty-five and responsible enough to deal with the money. I was anxious to get things settled, and unfortunately, it appeared to Connie that all I cared about was our mom's money.

I became uncomfortable dealing with my sister, knowing how much she despised me. The longer I had to keep bothering her about it, the worse I felt about the end result.

One of the life insurance policies was in my name, which made things even more complicated. Connie was in need of money for Isabella's savings bonds, so I sent her the exact change to equal what Mom wanted for the kids' bonds. As soon as I sent her the money, she cut me off.

I tried not to bother Connie because of her delicate condition: she was pregnant, and Mom had just died. The process of handling the will dragged out for about a month, and then everything was settled in December.

Then, the day after Christmas, Granny C. died. This was another money headache for us. My mother had written me a letter that stated very specifically that regardless of what my grandmother's will stated, my Uncle Nicholas agreed to set aside some money for Connie and me.

Even though Granny's will stated that Uncle Nicholas was to inherit everything of hers, he would privately divide the estate in half, and Mom's half was to be divided between my sister and me. My mother told me this on the phone, and she wrote it to me in a letter. I trusted my uncle to honor her wishes. Conscious of the fact that I'd come across as greedy to Connie, I didn't say anything to my uncle about Mom's letter regarding Granny's estate.

Uncle Nicholas made no mention of giving Mom's half to Connie and me, not even a monthly allowance toward bills or help with a down payment on a house. In fact, I went to a lawyer's office and signed a waiver stating that I knew I was not inheriting anything from this estate. I did that because I believed my uncle was an honest man and would honor my mother's wishes.

My uncle came to clear out Granny's house in preparation to sell it. I was offered all the furniture I wanted. Mom's friends managed to get a truck and deliver it to our new house. That was very generous of Uncle Nicholas, but I still didn't dare say anything about Mom's half because of my sister. It only made sense to wait patiently and hope that my Uncle would do the right thing.

We lived in Betty's beautiful four-bedroom house from October 1994 to June 1995. The neighborhood was getting rough, and there were a few structural things wrong with the house. My uncle never came through with Mom's half, and the landlady really didn't want to put any money into the house, so we decided to move.

The apartment we moved to was really too small for the six of us. It was still located on the north side, but it was in the business section. There were rodents that were very large, almost too large to be called mice. We lived in this apartment for about two months. Then John got us to move back to the complex where he soon got a job as the superintendent.

Edward started first grade in the Hamilton schools, in a special education class, but the apartment complex we moved to was located in the Dewitt school district. The new district didn't pay much attention to the paperwork or maybe they didn't receive it early enough, so for the first two weeks of class, Edward's first grade teacher didn't understand why he needed special education. Edward then started behaving badly, and the school made changes in his classroom setting.

In the spring, I was hotlined to CPS again. This time, Peggy's daughter Sandra was pissed off that her mother was babysitting my children on her birthday. She thought her mother had my kids way too much. I thought that when I took some time to myself, I could be a better parent. I didn't give any consideration, nor did John, as to whom we were leaving the children with, and Peggy rarely said "no" to watching them.

The report said that Patrick had an ear infection so bad that a green discharge was draining out of his ears and that I was afraid to take him to the doctor. The second part of the report was that Isabella had a diaper rash, which was raw and bleeding from the vagina. That was not true. She did a have diaper rash every couple of months that would get really awful, but I would take her to the doctor without hesitation.

The CPS worker was very nice. I explained that when Patrick had symptoms of an ear infection, I took him to the doctor. I explained that the same went for a diaper rash or any other medical problem with any of my kids. In fact, I was the parent who brought her children to the doctor almost on a weekly basis from November to April with sniffles, colds, ear infections, and whatever else may have been wrong. Luckily, the report was labeled "unfounded."

After almost a year at the apartment complex, John decided he wanted to move us again, and he started to look for another job and apartment. Patrick received money once a month because of his disability, and Edward had money coming in twice a month because of his disability and from his biological father's Social Security Disability.

The twins started kindergarten in September, and we decided to move back to Hamilton from the suburb. Patrick was going to require a very intense special education program. There were many elementary schools, and we were hoping all three children could attend the same school.

Edward was going to be in a class with seven other special education students and about sixteen regular education students. Patrick needed the same setting. The school district had a school that could meet the needs of both boys, and Monica would be attending the same school. Isabella would be home with me.

Chapter 19

Searching

It was January 1996, and my life was a big fat mess. I was lonely, depressed, my marriage was a wreck, my children were out of control, and I felt like I was in Hell every day. My husband and I were complete opposites and our ideas and goals in life were completely different.

I was lonely because I didn't have any friends. The only friend I did have, Peggy, had nine children, two grandchildren, and her own chaos to deal with on a daily basis. She and I were nothing alike: she smoked cigarettes, drank coffee all day long, was not married, and used vulgar language toward her children when she got angry.

I didn't smoke, drink coffee, I had been married for four years, and when I got mad at my kids, I would say, "I'm mad at you. Your behavior is not making me happy." It was unusual for me to use curse words. But I was so dependent on Peggy watching my kids and being a "friend" that I grew used to the way she talked. I ignored it.

My husband John was a perfectionist and together we were boring. Wherever we lived had to be clean all the time. It couldn't be cluttered or messy. After the twins were born, our pediatrician even made a comment for John not to worry about the cleanliness of the house, just to enjoy his family. John wanted a clean house, and I wanted to enjoy the children. We didn't have any friends or family over, but the house was always very clean.

My boredom got me depressed. It seemed as though I was happier when I was working. The training I took back in 1986 to be a home health aide kept me working part-time for agencies on and off over the years. I could only work if my childcare arrangements were in order. Unfortunately, this seldom was the case; I tended to work, quit, start another job, quit and repeat.

When my days were full, I was the happiest. I couldn't seem to be organized enough to entertain the children like a traditional mother. I struggled with balancing their schedules and working part-time. It was hard for me.

Edward was almost seven and just finishing first grade. He acted like a mini-Rambo sometimes. He played rough and enjoyed stirring things up a bit. The twins were almost five years old. They were pretty good and not too mischievous. Monica was more playful and liked to test John, to see what he would do. She was not into girlie things yet like playing with her hair or painting her nails, and she was not afraid to get dirty. She was also very smart.

I was looking forward to Monica's days being more educational and stimulating for her than her time spent at home with me. Patrick was a sweetie pie and very easy to please. He took naps and was a very good toddler. Patrick was still attending special education Pre-K for half the day and did very well. We were hoping for more progress, but the neurologist had stated he had a "non-specific neurological disorder."

This diagnosis gave Patrick the opportunity to receive speech therapy, occupational therapy, and physical therapy, starting at thirteen months old. He was not diagnosed with cerebral palsy or autism.

Isabella was one and a half. She was sweet, slept okay, and had more energy than the twins.

We lived in the large complex where John worked, but it was unpleasant for him to live and work in the same building. We moved seven times in the first five years we were married, mostly because we had difficulty coming up with the rent. We would find a cheaper place, wheel and deal with the landlord to get a deal on the security deposit, and then there'd always be something wrong with the apartment.

For the most part, we had really good reasons to move. There were a couple of times we moved into an area of the city we were unfamiliar with, only to find out it was an unsafe neighborhood, and then we would move immediately. It would make sense to ask a family member for help with a security deposit, but I just didn't have the nerve to ask.

I was lonely for more friends. I wanted a deeper relationship with John, and I wanted to be a better parent and raise the kids "right." To better put it, I wanted the kids to grow into healthy, successful, high-functioning adults.

Because I was so lonely, I began searching for God. I was visiting churches, and I was ready to find Him.

In March 1996, I gave my friend Alice a call. She was the manager I worked with at my first fast food restaurant job. I picked up the phone, desperate for someone to talk to.

"Hello?"

"Hi Alice! It's me, Emily. How are you?"

"I'm good! What's goin' on?"

I started with a big sigh and said, "John and I are moving again, John is changing jobs, the kids are wild, and my finances are—"

"Hold up, Emily. You sound miserable."

"Yes," I admitted, glad she couldn't see the look on my face.

"You can do something about that. There are scriptures in the Bible that tell us what we need to do to have a better life. My pastor is teaching on Mark 4:1-32." I was half listening and slightly rolling my eyes. "Listen, I have to go," she said. "I have Bible Study at 6:30 PM, and I should be home around 9:00 PM if you want to call me back, okay?"

"Yes, I might do that. Enjoy yourself."

"Okay, Emily. Hang in there. You know, it could be worse."

"Oh really? How?"

"Well, there are lots of people in this world who don't have half of what you do. You should be grateful."

"I know," I said in a whisper.

"I love ya. Call me later."

"Love you too. Bye now," I said, before hanging up the phone.

I didn't call Alice back that same night, but I thought hard about what she had said. I was hoping I would find my place as a woman, wife, and mother. But I was also looking for some sort of support so I wasn't stressed all the time.

I had been to a couple churches in the few months prior to my conversation with Alice and searching hard for God for about a year. Most of the churches I attended had been traditional, very specific, and held very organized worship services. The pastor picked a modern subject to lecture on and rarely made any reference to Jesus and how we could apply certain Bible stories to our own lives. They had about ten to twelve minutes to deliver their sermon.

The church where John and I were married had a very tall pastor with a deep monotone voice. I can't remember learning anything from his sermons or from the Bible study I attended. When I was dating Brett, I went to a children's second and third grade Sunday school where I was supposed to be an assistant, and I learned the story of creation in Genesis right along with students in class.

I thought I knew everything I wanted to know about religion and what I was supposed to do. But I was still searching for Him. I knew Psalm 23—or knew of it. I knew the story in Genesis, and I knew how the world was created. I also had memorized Genesis 1:1, but I was still lonely and my soul was still searching for God.

A few weeks went by, and I was worn down by our choice to move again. Edward would be changing schools, and Patrick was going to have a dynamic two-year special education plan set up for him outside the Hamilton School District. We were in the Dewitt School District now, and they worked hard to put goals and programming together for Patrick's special needs. The suburban schools didn't have kindergarten all day, so Patrick's educational needs would have to be stretched out over more time.

I called Alice up, again, to complain about my life.

"Hello," a deep voice answered.

"Hello, is Alice there?"

"Yes, hold on."

"Hello," Alice answered.

"Hi, it's Emily. Are you busy?"

"No, not right this second. What's up?"

"Nothing, just that we are moving again, and I am sick of moving. The kids are going into kindergarten in September, and Edward will be in second grade. Our money is never right and—"

"Okay, okay, Emily. You need a Bible."

"I do?"

"Yes, Psalm 23. And don't forget what I just told you a few weeks ago."

Almost ashamed, I said, "I know. Someone out there is worse off than me. I know."

"We have church service at 11:00 AM on Sundays; you should come and visit."

"Really? You will be there?"

"Yes, I'm usually there about fifteen minutes early."

"Okay, where is the church?"

"It's on the corner of Conklin and South Street—a big church on the corner. You'll see a bell in the yard. It's across the street from the kids' school; do you know where the school is?"

"Yes, we had a meeting there last week for Edward."

"Good. So come visit, and then you'll see what I mean. You have to apply scriptures to your life and trust the Lord."

"Yeah, I know."

"Yeah, you know," she said in a mocking tone. "Then why do you keep calling me up and complaining about your life?"

"It's funny you invited me to church because I have been visiting churches these last six or seven months—looking. So far, nothing has struck me yet. I hope your church is different."

"It's not about church, Emily. It's about the Lord in your life—your life at home, in front of your husband and children. It's about Jesus, not just church."

"Alright, I will see you Sunday. What should I wear?"

"Anything you want; there's no dress code. Wear whatever is comfortable for you."

"Thank you, Alice. See you this weekend."

"Okay, see you Sunday. Bye now"

"Bye."

Chapter 20

Forgiven

It was a week before Easter in 1996 when I decided to visit Alice's church. I didn't know what to expect, but I knew my soul was hungry. So I went for it.

It was a beautiful church, and the worship service started promptly at 11:00 AM. Alice was in the congregation, and I walked up behind her and tapped her on her shoulder. She turned around and gave me a big hug. The seats were slowly filling up.

A man walked up to me and said, "Good morning, it's nice to have you here."

He was an average height, bald, and had the kindest face I had seen in years. The congregation of the church was predominantly African American. I didn't care. I wanted to be with Alice, and I was searching for God. Maybe this was poetic justice for me.

The service began, and I sat next to Alice. The congregation stood up as the choir came down the aisle and started singing. People were already crying with their hands up in the air, shouting, *"Thank you Jesus! Praise the Lord!"* The choir sang with beautiful gospel voices. I had only heard that kind of singing briefly on television in a few movies (I thought of the scene at the end of *The Color Purple*).

There was an order of service in place, but notice was given in the bulletin that the service was "subject to change, by order of the Holy Ghost." After the choir introduced a song, the deacons were in charge of the worship and praise time. There was a devotional period of scripture being read, another song and prayer, then announcements, greeting of the visitors, more prayer, and the choir sang again. Finally, after an hour of scripture reading, prayer, and singing, the preacher gave his sermon.

The pastor was medium height and wore a robe. He was bald but looked like he was in his mid-thirties. He spoke directly from the scriptures. He gave a title to his sermon, introduced several points he was going to discuss, and went on to compare the story to everyday life. He broke it down further so everyone could understand what he was talking about. He preached for about forty-five minutes.

The very first sermon I heard him preach was about a short man who wanted to see Jesus so badly that he climbed up a sycamore tree to see Him. Jesus went over to the tree, looked up, and told the man to climb down right away. This is from the gospel of Luke, chapter nineteen, starting in verse one.

At the end of the sermon, there was more prayer and then an invitation to discipleship. At this time, I saw little elderly ladies go up to the front of the church and tell the pastor and congregation about the little things that God had done for them. They spoke of big things, too. They talked and talked, received applause from the congregation, kisses and hugs from the pastor, and then sat down.

At the end, right before the congregation was dismissed, the pastor made an announcement: "Let's treat next Sunday like any other Sunday and not get all dressed up."

Easter was a day I knew very little about. I thought I did, but truthfully, I knew absolutely nothing. At this church, men were very dressed up in suits and ladies wore fancy hats. I was the only woman in the congregation wearing pants. I was moved by the long, long church service. It gave me a peace that I could hardly describe in words. But I wasn't going to go to church on Easter, because I didn't have anything to wear. Even though the pastor said very specifically it was not about what you wear, that's not what I heard him say. I was afraid I wouldn't fit in.

I remember the Easter service when I lived in Waterville. We attended an Episcopal church. I had no clue about the Bible and what it said. This particular church service was very organized, and its services were almost routine.

I was in the choir, and I remember the whole service from beginning to end. During a certain part of the Easter church service, the priest put a paper rabbit on a silver plate, set it on fire and covered the plate. When he lifted it up, there was a live rabbit underneath. After the service was over, the rabbit was raffled off and given away. Also, during a certain part of the service, you heard a loud thump. It was the young people standing or getting up and looking under the pew's cushions for chocolate eggs and jellybeans. I don't remember anything about the true meaning of Easter at church as a young person.

I went to Alice's church again. It was the Sunday after Mother's Day. The same kind man greeted me again when I walk in the door.

When all the devotional time, prayer, announcements, and choir singing were over, the preacher preached again. This time it was Mark 5:25-34, about a woman who had "the issue of blood" for twelve years. It was a great test of faith for this young woman who had been to see many doctors after bleeding for twelve straight years, only to be cured by touching the hem of Jesus' robe. The pastor was adamant about giving our issues, problems, and worries to the Lord. He would take care of everything, and we should always trust Him. "We need to know the Lord for ourselves," he said.

Again, I left the service with an overwhelming sense of peace. And again, I was at a loss for words to describe how I was feeling. I didn't have a Bible, but I was happy to visit this church once every two to three weeks. I was very relieved because I thought I had found God. So far, I had attended church just a few times and enjoyed the pastor's sermons. But I didn't get the salvation part yet.

We moved out of the complex back to Hamilton from Dewitt, to a very big three bedroom on the first floor of a two-family house. It was on the inner city's West End. John had changed jobs again, and we were preparing for the kids to start school soon.

On a Tuesday in June 1996, the kids and I were all home. It was afternoon, and we were resting. At least, I thought the kids were all resting, but apparently Patrick was not. He got up and found my car keys, went outside to where my car was parked in the driveway, opened the door, and sat in the driver's seat. Patrick put my keys in the ignition and put the car in reverse. The car rolled backward and out of the driveway, across the street.

Sometime around 2:00 PM, the doorbell rang. I got up without putting on my eyeglasses and opened the front door. An older gentleman was at the door, and Patrick was standing next to him. He asked me, as he pointed across the street, "Is that your car?"

I couldn't really see it at first, and I said, "No, I don't think so."

"Are you sure?"

I said, "Hold on, let me get my glasses." I stepped away from the front door and got my glasses on. I returned to the front door and looked across the street. I could see my car just slightly over the curb and within an inch of another car.

"Oh my God!" I gasped.

The man said, "It's okay, Miss. I found this boy in the car; everything is okay."

I asked the man to stay there with Patrick while I moved the car back to the driveway, and he did. I thanked him many times over for bringing Patrick across the street, and he left.

This was the incident that changed my life forever. It was obvious that God was trying to get my attention, and He did. My car didn't hit the parked car across the street. It missed it by two or three inches. The interstate on-ramp was a block away, and no cars were coming down the street when Patrick backed out of the driveway. He could have been killed, but his life was spared.

John came home about two hours later from work, and I told him what happened. The next day, as soon as the stores opened, we purchased double-keyed locks for the front and back door. I made sure I had my keys with me at all times, in case of an emergency.

John and I decided to avoid the family center for a couple of weeks after this happened, and I didn't open my big mouth to anyone, except Peggy.

It was a miracle that Patrick was safe after backing the car out into the street and that no one called Child Protective Services or the police. This experience led me to go back to Alice's church again. When the time was coming up for an invitation to discipleship, I planned on going up front to tell the congregation about how good God was to me. I didn't realize that before I went up in front of the congregation, there was a specific way I was supposed to join the church. I was missing out because I didn't attend Sunday school or Bible study yet.

The head pastor was not there that day, and one of the assistant ministers preached in his place. I had another great time in church and paid attention. I felt full of joy!

The invitation to discipleship came at the end of the service. I wanted to go up and tell what happened. I didn't understand yet about salvation and discipleship. But because I saw the elderly ladies go forward and talk about how good God had been to them, I thought I could do that as well. This was my plan; however, this was not God's plan.

Someone was appointed every Sunday to record who came forth at the invitation, as well as why they had come forth. Sister Secretary came and sat next to me with the record book in her hand. She asked me my name, and before I could tell her that I wanted to testify, she asked me, "Do you want to be a candidate for baptism?"

I didn't know the vocabulary yet for what I wanted to do, which was to testify.

I answered, "Yes."

I didn't get to say anything about my son or his near-death accident that made me turn to God completely. I knew that being baptized again meant all the stuff I did would be forgiven, but I still didn't know the salvation part yet.

Life was not the same as it was before my four-year-old backed the car out into the street. After two Sundays went by, I ran into a sister who recognized me and said, "Are you coming Sunday to be baptized?"

I responded with, "Oh, okay; it's this Sunday?"

The following Sunday, I returned to church for the 5:00 PM service. This was the once-a-month scheduled baptism service. The service included song, prayer, some preaching, and usually at least three people were baptized. This was also the service where the church offered communion to believers. I was a little nervous and happy at the same time.

There were four of us to be baptized. The mothers, deaconesses, and women missionaries of the church were in the bathroom getting me ready. They pinned my hair up and put a shower cap on my head. They also wrapped me in a white sheet, and I wore white socks. The four of us sat in the front row of the sanctuary.

I was the third person to be baptized. I went up the steps when it was my turn and waited to be told to go down in the water. When that time came, I crossed my arms and closed my eyes while the pastor prayed for me, my household, and my new life with Christ.

"I baptize you in the name of the Father, the Son, and the Holy Ghost," he said, assisting me under the water and back up again. I walked to the other end of the pool and got out of the water. I was now a baptized believer and forgiven by God for all the rotten stuff I had done in the last thirty-one years and four months of my life.

I had finally found the unconditional love of Jesus Christ. I felt for the first time that my life was brand new. I was at peace with my life, and that was just the beginning. I knew my life would never be the same.

II Corinthians 5:17-21 applies to me as a baptized believer. All the things that I ever said—the lies, the hate, the racism, the bad jokes—all is forgiven by God. All the things I did—using men for sex, lying to them, teasing them, and not respecting myself—all is forgiven by God. Everything I did to my family—lying to, stealing from, and using my mother and sister, as well as my rebellious teen years of being ungrateful, greedy, selfish, etc.—all is forgiven by

God. All that I did to my immediate family and friends—John and his family, my children, Edward and his father, Monica, Patrick and Isabella—all is forgiven by God.

When I was in that pool of water, I asked God for His forgiveness for all the bad things I had done. When I came up out of the water, I knew I was forgiven; I had a fresh start as a new believer.

Alice walked up to me after the baptism and communion service was over, and we talked for a few minutes.

"Congratulations, Emily," Alice said.

"Thank you! I'm so excited."

"Do you want to come over my house tonight?"

"Sure, that would be great."

"Okay, I have some juice and snacks we can munch on and talk. You know where I live?"

"Yes, I'll see you in about fifteen minutes; I just have to run home and tell John, okay?"

"Okay, see you in a few."

I went home and asked John if he would stay with the kids while I went over to Alice's house for a couple of hours, and he said yes. Alice said it was okay to bring Edward over. He could watch TV or play with the dog.

I drove over to Alice's with Edward. It was a pleasant evening outside for the first weekend in July. It wasn't too hot at all. Edward was a little shy, but he sat at the table and ate a piece of watermelon while Alice and I talked.

Alice asked me, "So, how are you feeling?"

"Pretty good. I like the church."

"Did you get a Bible?"

"Yes, they are mad cheap at Family Dollar. I got the King James version for five dollars, and I have been marking the pages with a yellow highlighter when the pastor teaches."

"Good for you, that's great."

"Sometimes you have to wait for family. It's a process for everybody."

"I know. I'm just so excited; I can't believe it," I said with a huge smile on my face. "Now I have this huge, huge family, and we are going to be all right."

"Yeah, but just be careful and know that there may be hard times. Don't get confused when bad things happen."

"I won't. I'm just sorry my mom isn't alive so I could apologize to her. I'm sorry I can't apologize to my sister—she never returns my calls or letters. I was really a terrible teenager and young adult."

"Have you read Romans 3:23? I don't know anyone who is perfect but Jesus Christ Himself. Just because you are baptized now and a new believer, doesn't mean you're perfect. People aren't going to believe you; they will question you and may come up against you. That's the first thing I noticed as a new believer."

"What did you notice?"

"People expect you to act perfect. And trust me, sometimes the flesh gets the best of me, too."

"The flesh? What do you mean?"

"You are saved, but your flesh is not saved. So, if you are in a long, long line at a fast food restaurant and someone cuts in front of you, that's not very nice, right?

"Right," I agreed.

"So, your natural reaction—your flesh—would be to mouth off and say something. But now, as a new believer, you should ignore them; that's acting Godly. Does that make sense?"

"Yeah, I guess so. So no more having temper tantrums or feeling sorry for myself."

"There you go; that's right. And you are accountable for your choices and behavior. You can no longer blame everybody else for your bad situations and your bad choices."

"But, some things are not my fault," I replied.

"Aww, no more! You must take responsibility."

"Yeah, you're right. What else do I need to know?"

"Get yourself to Bible study on Wednesday nights and Sunday school at 9:30 AM on Sunday mornings. As a new believer, you'll be in the Foundations class."

"Oh, okay, and bring the kids too?"

"Not at first. You come by yourself at first, get used to everything, and then bring them. Or yes, bring them right away. They have Sunday school for them too and Junior church on Bible study night as well."

"I didn't have a bad childhood, you know?"

"Why do you say that?" Alice asked.

"Well, even though my parents got married, divorced, remarried, and divorced, and then my mom did the same thing with her second husband, we still had everything we needed. We moved a lot. But Mom tried very hard to raise us right. I failed her; she didn't fail me. I don't want to make the same mistakes with my children."

"You won't. You have to trust God. You can't just trust Him or call on Him when you need something. And sometimes, Emily, don't tell everybody everything. Sometimes we have to be quiet and keep things to ourselves, pray about it, and let the Lord fight our battles for us."

"Oh my gosh! That worker I had, Roxy—she was a Christian like us. She would be so happy to find out that I am too. And Linda and Mary, my second cousins, are Christians, too, and they'll will be so surprised to find out."

"That's great. Don't stop praying for people in your family. One day it might happen for them too. Share what you know, read your Bible, come to church, and pray. Those are the four primary things to do as a new believer."

"It's getting late; we better get going."

Edward was in a chair watching cartoons, and he looked like he was falling asleep. Alice had cable, and we didn't. Edward usually watched movies at home but not cartoons too often.

"Okay honey, do what is right and call me anytime."

We exchanged hugs, and she gave Edward a hug as well. I got in the car and drove away. On the way home, Edward was quiet. I was quiet, too, and for me, that was a first. I had a lot to think about.

THE HITCH HIKER/TEXAS

From Nothing To Something

HITCH HIKER

iUniverse, Inc.
Bloomington

THE HITCH HIKER/TEXAS
FROM NOTHING TO SOMETHING

iUniverse books may be ordered through booksellers or by contacting:

iUniverse
1663 Liberty Drive
Bloomington, IN 47403
www.iuniverse.com
1-800-Authors (1-800-288-4677)

ISBN: 978-1-4620-3439-0 (pbk)
ISBN: 978-1-4620-3506-9 (ebk)

Printed in the United States of America

iUniverse rev. date: 07/11/2011

CONTENTS

THIS BOOK IS DEDICATED

"TO PEOPLE AND CHILDREN WITHOUT A SONG, A
SONG THAT'S SUPPOSE TO KEEP
THEM ALIVE, A SONG CALLED,
"EVERYTHING I NEED TO SURVIVE"

TO THOSE WHO GOT LOST ON THE WAY TO
THEIR FUTURE, BECAUSE OF NEVER HAVING
THE SUPPORT OF THOSE THAT KEPT IT
AWAY FROM THEM,

AND I HOPE THAT I CAN MAKE A
DIFFERENCE IN SOME PEOPLE'S LIVES BY
GIVE SOMETHING BACK FINANCIALY, TO
MAKE SOME OF YOU HAPPIER WITH A
BETTER FUTURE.

IF YOU DO READ ONE OF MY BOOKS AND I CAN'T
GET TO YOU, PLEASE STAND UP AND GO INTO YOUR
FUTURE TO HELP YOURSELF AND TAKE SOME OF YOUR
FRIENDS WITH AS A TEAM, I BELIEVE THAT YOU WILL
MAKE IT IF YOU CHOOSE TO MAKE IT. "BUILD YOUR
OWN SONG."

"HITCH HIKER"

ABOUT THE AUTHOR

A practical person who will travel the world to change the future of people that never got the opportunity to build a future for them selves.

He chose to make it part of his life to create better opportunities into other peoples lives for one reason; "he know how it feels to be in a situation with no help as a child."

That's why he made a choice to invest some of his profit of all his books into some of these people, especialy children in need.

Special thanks to; **Seatle Coffee Company** in Menlyn centre and Brooklyn mall Pretoria South Africa, for make it possible to sit and write on this special stories to send into the world.
I enjoyed the Caffe Latte's, thankyou.
Also thanks to **Dross restaurant** in Menlyn centre for some nice pizzas.

"HITCH HIKER"

Everybody was born, and we are not responsible for that decision, sad case most of the time. Some people are born without a future plan from their parents. Every couple wants a child, but nobody make the sum into the future; it cost a little more what they bargain for, as a matter of fact millions more if you look at the financial side.

Whether we like it or not, we are born and here we are. You can get born on the high way or on the gravel road, smooth or rough beginning.

If you are born on the rough terrain, you will be most of the time one of the toughest persons around, if you make it? if you are born in some areas in Africa, South America, India or one of these crowded countries or continents you will really be a winner if you reach the grown up world, but the real winner will be the one who left his circumstances and become a leader in his area or elsewhere by using his life choices very carefully.

What makes it sometimes more difficult is the fact that when it doesn't work out for parents, they will find a way to get rid of children, because they can't look after themselves financially. Luckily for them some governments created orphanages for children like us. All of the children have lost their parents, whether

1

it's because of an accident or other circumstances. Orphanage are one of the oldest shelters for children in the world, not a nice place to be, but at least a roof over the head and food to eat. Today I look at the modern orphenages in the first world, called chreches; they will drop their children in the morning and pick them up in the evening.

No more mothers at home to learn the children about the basics of life only a mother can do. Higher standards, tea parties and and and no children.

Unfortunately I have landed in one of these orphanages in the early sixties, today in 2011 it's a much better atmosphere, people are more caring over children in some first world countries today, **it's sad to see a child sad, it's like a bird with no song, tree with no shade, a cloud with no rain, country with no leader . . . .**

BUT, we are born with choices, "MILLIONS" of them and that's one piece of freedom they can't take away from us. Choices, choices, choices, to stay where you have started, or to make a choice to move on to your heart's desire, new positive levels that can make you a new person, a leader you maybe have dreamed of for many years, or not. Choices are there for every individual on this planet. But, it's the individual's choice if he or she wants to take it or not. **(Stay behind, or go into your future that awaits you)**

This is not a book to tell you about all of my life, because some parts of our lives must stay our own, it has got nothing to do with other people. Things you must treasure close to your heart.

I struggled through life with nothing, only my choices someone builded into me before I arrived in this practicle world, the world of choices, something people can't build into a human being. We received it on our birthday and it's been given with no price on it, we received it for free, its very importend that we must discover the millions of choices we received and use it in a positive way, a way to help others to survive as well. "THINK BEFORE YOU MAKE USE OF YOUR CHOICES"

My name: John van der Schyff, born on 11th December on the African continent in a country called SOUTH AFRICA, city Pretoria.

Some of you will remember South Africa for the soccer world cup that was held here in 2010, and the winners were Spain, just in case you forgot.

I am writing this book for a couple of reasons, **1)** to motivate some of you out there, maybe you are in the same position I was in. **2)** to tell you that there's always a process in life we must go through, you must do your homework to get somewhere after the choice you have made. **3)** I don't want to take my true life story with me to the grave one day. **4)** To put some of this books profit into people that need it to survive. **5)** to let you know that your choice will bring some things to your life in the future you haven't planned for. **(6** that you can look after your own family and many other families long after you have left this earthly world by leaving behind the right choice or choices you have made for those that must stay behind.

My life started as one of those thrown away kids at the age of three.

I don't blame the parents for their mistakes they have made in my life, they're just human and not perfect but, I blamed God for many years, because of the fact that He says in his word, He is the creator of all things, so then He must be the responsible one. I don't understand this world, but I made a decision many years ago and I'm still on it, mistakes or not, I must keep on going, nobody else will do it on my behalf.

I remember the times sitting at the orphanage window during the day, looking at the road that was running past the orphanage, with the hope that somebody will come and give me a visit, just someday. No success.

The man that stands at the door in the morning with his cane in his hand forcing the children out of the hall morning by morning, a picture I will never forget.

The brown porridge in the morning, day after day, I cut that porridge with peace out of my life forever.

The time I kicked my right big toe against a rock and lost my big toe nail, nobody there to put a arm around a three year old boy and to wipe his new tears of his feature face. I can still feel that heart desire pain today after so many years.

So one day somebody came for me, a family with three children, little girl my age, middle one also a girl two years older, and then the oldest one a boy six years older than me. Sometimes we must watch out what we're dreaming for. My dream became a reality but a nightmare, how could that be possible? Three spoiled brats, everything they say you must do, from the mother to the youngest one.

One day I ignored the youngest ones instruction and got a black board thrown at me, the corner of the board cut me under my left eye, blood all over my feature face. They took me to hospital for my first stitches, more of those to come later in my life, and I can't count the stitches on the scars in my heart, there's too many to count, normally it's our filing cabinet that's the problem, *"the brain"*, if we can make peace in our filing cabinet we will make it.

Not allowed in the house during the day, you must get your food at the window during the day, got my water from the outside toilet as a four year old during the day. **(Remember I'm white)**

I remember the time I was so hungry while playing in the sand, I saw a piece of dry bread in the sand, I put it in my mouth to cure the hunger pain in my stomach, hard as a rock, but who cares it helped me forget my need for a while.

I never had the support to build self confidence at this beginning of my life, never had friends, I couldn't communicate *with others, too shy to ask questions if I* don't understand something.

From an early age I have started to build a type of self discipline into my life, to help me to cope with things I don't want in my life, things that will break my body down. I discover one thing that I must treasure, and that's my body, if I can look after it, I will survive much longer and can be much stronger when life itself attacks me with things I didn't plan.

Doing sports, run where ever I go, and of cause a good diet, think before I put something into my body, and the amount to.

I struggled through school, college and then one day I met a person that changes my whole life around forever. He had a sport centre, and invited me to join his practice sessions; I went one session and kept on going for five yours. Became one of the best students, why? Because I wanted to be the best, but the positive about this decision I have made, is the fact that he build self confidence into my life that I never had and knew will help me to survive in the future that awaits me.

To become a *"HITCH HIKER"* with passion in a country for people on highways that's been pushed out by churches, politics, parents and their own mistakes, mistakes they can't tell anybody about of, not even their best friend, a baggage they carry around called their past, the only past and future we allowed to carry with us must be the one with peace written all over it. They only needed a friend for the time I were in their vehicle, just enough time for them to get this burden of their hearts, they knew they're not going to see this hitch hiker again, lets offload. It was good to see people going away with freedom, people that feel they received a second change. Every human being has the right to be free.

It's on one of this hitch hiking trips that I had one of the most scary but successful stories on the road. I got a short lift with a motorist in a town early in the morning where he dropped me just outside the town onto the main road to the south, on my way to Cape Town.

I put my bag next to the road like all the previous times, but this morning it's different, as if the atmosphere is just right for something good to happen. I got my book out and carry on reading from where I last stopped, don't like the idea of putting my arm out to get a lift, the motorist must choose to pick me up, while I keeping myself busy reading, not to look at them as a beggar for a lift, times on my side, if I get to Cape Town in three days time, I don't care, I'll get there, **patients.** The time went by, one hour, two hours, at the fifth hour a yellow Ford pickup with scrap metal on the back stopped very slowly in front of me, the driver opened the window and offered me a lift. I put my bag on top of the scrap metal and got in next to him. We took off.

We made friends in about half an hour time, a twenty six year old mail with good standards, a person that can keep a conversation alive. As we exchange our pasts and future, he asked me the next question, "do you know the reason I picked you up". "not really I answered", he carried on, before I stopped in front of you, I was busy planning to shoot myself, because I'm bankrupt, and don't know how to carry on in life anymore," he pulled a silver revolver from his jacket and showed it in my direction. He started to wept, tears running from his cheeks, (something I know very well in my life, tears) when a person is at this level you can help him by bringing in words of motivation to color in his future with positive pictures, pictures he will understand to turn his circumstances around so that he can see a light up future for himself again.

That's the way it went with this bankrupt motorist on that specific day, we drove for five hours before he dropped me in the darkness. He left with a greatfull heart with only one word in it, POSITIVE!!

I spoke to him six months after that nearly disastres day, I couldn't believe it's the same person I'm talking to. He was telling me about his new job, and where ever his going his picking up hitch hikers to motivate them in their situation they're in.

"I was born in a state called Texas in the USA on the 11th December, my name, Tephany Parker nick name "Angel" my father's name to his beautifull daughter, his only child and his Angel."

I got everything in life, rich parents, oil brought in money by the millions. My father looked after me in a way other children and parents could only dream of.

I enjoyed the cream of this world, best of everything you can think of, clothes, shoes, room to sleep in that looks like an angel's room, my own bank account from an early age. My father learned me about money many children off my age didn't know, and I'm good in it, he made me part of his business from the age of six. So I learned about the business side, he often said, "Angel you must know where money comes from, that brings balance in your life."

On my 5th birthday my father bought me the most beautiful black stallion, "Fresh". I loved that horse, a friendship I can't explain to you. "Fresh" helped me escape from my pain after my mothers accident. My father knew that he must keep me busy and did the right thing to buy me a horse. There is just something special between man and horse that will stay forever on this planet. Fresh learned me a lot about staying calm. If I need to get away, I will take "Fresh" and ride him for many kilometers away from our house, we will sit next to the river that flows through our farm, and just be myself. It's next to this river I have made one of my biggest decisions of my life that will bring me in a future I never dreamed of.

I became part of the farms, because I like to be in nature, helping with the cattle, feeding the horses, cleaning the stables, I just liked to be part of the outside world. My clothes were always dirty at the end of the day. If there's an emergency situation at night I will be part of it.

My father made sure that I must be with him one day in the week to learn about his oil business.

We would fly sometimes over the farm to look at his kingdom and to look for water leaks on the water pipelines that lead from the river to the maize lands.

One thing about my father, his very accurate, because of his discipline, he doesn't give you much tollerance in life. I never found the grey area in his life, and I missed it a lot, only right or wrong counts for him.

I enjoyed being with my dad in the beginning of my life, but it grew into a business relationship that smashed the whole father daughter relationship into million pieces later in my life. I needed a father not a business partner like a man can only dream of, he made sure to train me about the basics of business during all these years, so that I can run his whole business on the age of sixteen, and even fly his plane, checking the cattle and water pipelines, or just for the fun of it, I love to fly.

My father had a plan with me, and it worked out for him, but he missed something over all these years, something I discovered when I turned sixteen, a fathers love. I did miss something over the years but couldn't put my finger on it, till that one day next to the river; I was sitting on the green grass while "Fresh" was drinking water from the river. I went back home that day as another person, a person that has made a new and radical decision for a new future, a person with a desire for her husband one day in the future, and peace over my situation with my father and our relationship. Peace right in the centre of my heart. I'm free.

I looked at him one day, and saw something I don't wanted to see, only a business partner. All our conversations, business trips, flying in the plane, business, business, business . . . . But I love him just the way he is; he was the only man in my life for a long time. Don't miss it, he is a great dad, brilliant leader, but I never felt this love from him as a father between father and daughter. Think you know what I'm talking about."

I never had the graze for men, of cause a couple of them tried their luck, but if you know me better you will keep your distance, and to back me up, a father with a look you wouldn't like coming your way. People respect him and the younger ones will keep a distance. He always has an answer on any question."

I need a man that knows nothing about my back ground; he must exept me without asking or knowing anything about me, nothing, a man with a heart not a face. He must except me as a person, not because of my looks and back ground, a hornets man with a vision, a thinker with tenderness.

I never had, someone that will touch me whether I need it or not. A man that can come into my life in an area I never allowed any man in.

I need a man to bond with that area, a area I want to give away with no price on it, it's not business, it's called love, you can't plan it, you don't know when and where, sounds scary but right. If I meet someone like this I know I will give my all forever.

Maybe one day there will be someone like that, maybe one day.

At the age of sixteen I got everything I needed to go into a future without any help from anybody on this earth. Nobody knew that, why? Because we're use to things, and I'm a practical person, I just want to be a plain girl without success tags. Butt . . . .

What will a woman be without a husband and her own family, husband to be with, to do things with, to tell special things to, to lay with, next to a fire place under a blanket, to sleep with, to play with, and children to look after???

I have made a decision next to the river that day to picture my husband in my mind and on the right age I will go and look for him, if he hasn't arrive before that time. I will be able to leave everything behind if necessary. I kept this secret close to my heart and longed for the day when I'm going to meet this special person, I could feel him already, I knew from that day next to the river his out there somewhere.

Now there are two men in my life, my father and my husband, and I don't even know how my husband looks like, but I know we will be great friends, no friendship, means no husband. He will be gentle and passionate, a family man. A man that will know what he wants in a woman, his friend, wife and partner for life.

It's sad to look at my father and see him in the shade, there's someone new in my life I can look up to, he looks like a person with softness in his face I haven't seen before, a caring and tenderness that shines from his face, I like what I'm seeing, it gives me a feeling of security I don't know, but enough peace to accept it, my heart feels like a mountain. The second day after my river decision, my father wanted to know what's wrong with me.

"You are not concentrating Angel, you must listen when I explain things to you, I want you to focus."

"But I knew for the first time in my life, that things are rite, I feel so good, so damn good. It's as if something in my heart exploded and my heart feels much bigger than before, so peacefull.

The birds are singing new songs today, I think, the clouds are . . . . I am changing I feel that I'm in the clouds, what a new feeling."

I worked very hard for the next couple of years on the farms, especially on my own farm, from the entrance to the garden, the house and all the detail you can think off, but I kept it simple, like me, I left all the extra rooms white and empty, the rooms for our children, that we will plan together, I feel that is the right thing to do, our own ideas together for every child. I like a farm house not a city house on a farm, it's not me, and I'm hundred percent sure this is what my feature husband will want too. If not, I'm willing to change it, but at least it keeps me busy with a dream.

I build a nice tree house next to the river wit a thatch roof and small fire place, just for us. (my fater helped me with the inspection while the contracters were building the tree house, because I know his very precisely and accurate when it comes to buildings as well.) A place we can escape to when we feel like it. I let them installed a lift that works with a winch, once you up there nobody can get up without the lift, nice and private.

One day while thinking about my husband, I saw something that went through my heart like a love arrow," brown hair". I'm busy getting the picture of my future husband, my love for him grew much stronger from that day on, the desire to meet him grew and I can't control it, I had to discipline my feelings not to get into my vehicle to go and look for him, but where will I go?

I dived into my work just more, and at night time I will fall asleep with this big peace smile on my face, I bought a big pillow and a couple of blue pillow sheets with the words "MY MAN" on it to hold at night, (training to hold my husband one day.)

On the age of twenty three, I was one of the strongest women in the Taxes business world, and my father one of the happiest persons in the world. I brought in new ideas in to the business and made millions extra every year, he smiled all the way.

Our relationship stayed the same all these years. I became the person that ran his whole business, with him only sitting in the meetings to keep tread with the growing of the company. The fact that I concentrate totally on my work during the day, kept men away in my life, if they do try to start a none business conversation, I will just ask them questions about business I know they can't answer and that will push them away out of my personal circle.

On weekends I will go to the river and sleep in our tree house, sit on the green grass during the day and wonder what it will be feel like to be married,? for me I'm already married for seven years, and still enjoy it like that first day I made that decision seven years ago. But I still need the closeness of a person to make it perfect. I have learned so many patience by thinking of my husband, and wonder where will he be at that moment, is he thinking of his future wife like I do about him as my husband?

As a fit sport instructor I moved to a town called East London in the Eastern Cape in South Africa. I had this nice five level town house, not close to the sea, but I could see the sea in a distance. I kept myself busy with road running and my bicycle. On weekends I will get into my wet suit and collect some mascles from the rocks to make some mascles and vegetable mixture topped with cheddar cheese.

I'm not fussy about food, but a barbecue on the fire and potato salad can chance an evening in something unstoppable.

I do get lonely at times, and it's in this Eastern Cape town I made a decision that will bring me in places that will fit my heart like a glove, a decision that will bring a richness into my life in many ways.

It came to a day in my life that everything just got too much for me. My past pushed me into a corner I couldn't get away from, I just had it with this world someone created and left us as humans to run it with so many pain in. How is it possible to make it with all this baggage of the past that follows us into our future? I hated my past with all the hate I could find in my heart.

There is something missing and I must find it. I packed my bag and drove for many kilometers just to get away for a weekend, as I get to a guesthouse thousand kilometers away from my place, I suddenly know what I have missed all the time about my passed. **Peace**. I must make peace before I can move on in my life. I took my bag got into my vehicle and drove all the way back to

East London. I cried for many hours on my way back to my town house, but for the first time in my life I knew what to do.

I got to my townhouse with this peace in my heart about the past and the future. One big mountain in my life was the fact that I had a god that anchored me in life, "my earthly things."

It's not wrong to have things in this world, but if it's your god you will never be your own boss. We must have control over things on this earth.

I've made a list of everything in the townhouse and advertise the whole lot, everything were gone in three weeks. I had only my car, some of my clothes, my backpack and cash on my name, but in my heart I have a desire to find people in need. I travelled by car to find hitch hikers on the high ways of South Africa. I just felt this urge in my heart to look after them. I made a decision to never of load them if they not at a safe place, and try to give them supplies to carry on for a couple of days.

I learned so much from these people with a future that's very bleak; I thought I had nothing, until I met them with only feet to walk with and maybe one meal for that day only.

I looked after the hitch hikers till I understood their way, but I never felt the way they feel. So I decided become one of them, I took my backpack and travel by foot to help the motorist country wide.

"**I** had another dream last night, I saw my husband with the peace full face, and I can still not see the picture of his face, but I saw some blood underneath his left eye, there's a cut and the blood and tears is running down his cheek dripping onto a black floor, but his not moving, there's no pain on his face, just peace.

From now on I have the picture of him with brown hair, cut under the left eye, and the peace shining from his face, and I know his looking straight at me, waiting like I do, busy but waiting for the day we going to meet, full of patience. I wept with him for that whole day, I had this pain in my heart for him, when I think about him during that day, my tears will just run out of my eyes, and I can't keep one of them back, and I didn't want to. I could feel his pain deep in my heart. Maybe I'm helping him carrying his pain, yes that must be it. I'm feeling much better after discovering that I'm part of his pain.

I can feel how my love for him is growing in my heart over the years, his taller than I am medium but well build.

Weekends in the tree house I will have conversations with him about the weeks work and things that worries me, I believe his a good listener, and I feel good after a conversation with him. I never had conversations with anybody like this in my life, also a new area I discovered in me, I can feel him coming closer and closer in my life every day and it makes my heart bounce like a ping pong ball. I feel so good.

I'm looking forward to the day we going to meet, it's going to be very special, like two people that will merge into one love bubble, and they will bubble of to a future only they will be happy in, a future full of harmony, and I know we will be happy.

I'm turning twenty eight on the 11 of December, two months to go, and decided to travel from New York to Texas for two months, November and December, I will fly to New York (because I looove New York) and stay there for my first week and then travel by car to enjoy the sceneries back to Texas and go from city to city to do one thing I always wanted to do, helping orphanages financially where ever I can find them. I have printed special voucher for them where they can only fill the name of the orphanage in and collect the food they need monthly.

I haven't been on holiday for the last eight years and think I need to get away for a while. My father agreed to look after the businesses and my farm. There are enough workers to do the work anyway, he must just check on them.

My travelling in South Africa as a hitch hiker took me through situations, situations that are too rough for the human on the long run; you will just not be able to make it if you carry on too long, the sun, rain, wind and on your feet most of the day, sleeping in the bush, sometimes rain you can't stop, pouring for hours, under high way bridges in the Karoo. Lifts in cars, trucks, in and on the back of pick-ups, you must keep your peace, peace, peace. Vision.

South Africa is one of the countries with the most beautiful nature sceneries in the world. If you travel in an area like the eastern side called Mpumalanga you will see some of the most beautiful waterfalls in nature. I stopped at one of these waterfalls with the name "Mac Mac falls" on my way to the east, as I walked back to the main road I saw a name someone engraved on one of the steps,

"Tephany," what a nice name I thought for a second as I strole towards the main road to get a position for my last lift for the day,

It's a pleasure to be in this pine tree forest, it's so easy to breath here, no vehicle fumes.

I made my thirty kilogram bag stand next to the road and wait for a Samaritan to pick me up. I never knew where I'm going to sleep at night, depend on my lifts during the day, if I'm not getting to a town at night, I will use my two men tent to sleep in, I will walk twenty or thirty meters into the bush get my tent nicely in position slip into my sleeping bag and use my bag as a pillow. My thoughts went back to think about the day and the waterfall, the name "Tephany" came up as well, and I fell into a deep sleep.

What will hitch hiking without nature? I travelled as a hitch hiker for thousands of kilometers through South Africa and Namibia the amount of kilometers I can't tell you, seen some places I can't tell you about in detail, there's too much detail in every place I've been to, I met wonderfull people on my journeys, it's better for you to take a couple of months of, to pack your vehicle and travel from town to town and city to city to experience something that will enrich you for your whole life money can't buy. If you do your planning well, you get through it very cheap.

I always wanted to go to America, I saw so much about America in the movies. In the sixty's, seventy's and eighty's you will only find American movies in South Africa, Chips, Trinity and Bud Spencer and, and, and, nothing from Europe, but you will get some movies from the east, Bruce Lee and some other kickers. I heard the song New York, New York, sang by a "blue eye singer" I think.

I think I'm on my way to see for myself what's going on in America, the country that's doing so much to help other poor countries, and also in the news for doing so much bad things as well, sending his people to other countries to get killed by the thousands. Why?

I will fly to New York and hitch hike down to Texas, one of the hurricane states of America, maybe I can find some work on farms to know the Texan people better, and to top up my dollars. The people in Texas have the funniest accent, they look like real cowboys.

My plane ticket are booked for the first week in November and planned to come back on the 3rd of January the next year. Two months will be long enough to see some of America. So, my birthday will be in America in a nice coffee shop on the 11th of December somewhere, depends on where I will be at that stage, if it's not too expensive I will buy coffee for everybody in the coffee shop.

"Yes, that's what I will do for my special day."

"My birthday in America."

It feels good to be sitting in this chair up in the sky; it's like a miracle, in a piece of metal thousands of feet above the earth. The last plane landed twenty four hours later on JF Kennedy airport after I got on the first plane in South Africa. I'm tired.

My father took me to the airport; we are use to flying, so it's like a business trip for him, but for me it's a holiday, I planned my whole trip months ago, this is the way I am, everything in detail, that's me, detail counts a lot, it's something special in my life, planning. I have this expectancy, maybe I feel like this because I haven't been on holiday for so many years.

I closed my eyes and can feel how the speed pushes me backwards into the seat as the plane lifts of, I'm on my way. New "York, New York."

I took a yellow cab to my favorite hotel and just lay on the bed for a while; "I look at my watch, already 21h15, closed my eyes and woke up some time in the early hours of the next morning for the first time, I hate to go to bed without showering, I looked at the time 2 am. I get rid of my clothes and forced myself into the shower, will shower again before I go into the streets of New York, must shower every morning and evening, it's like eating, part of my life, will maybe bath once a month, too much in a hurry to take a bath, shower's much quicker and nicer.

Today will be a coffee shop day, my favourite place for doing nothing with a book in my hand and thinking of my future husband, "my husband, maybe I will meet him in New York . . . . ???????" I like this man; no, I love this man. I'm going to meet "MY MAN" one day.

I got out of my hotel at about 08.30, today no yellow cab, I'm not in a hurry, and I'm on holiday. Food, I need some food for this body, every time I get in New York I will get a coffee and a baycal and later a coffee and blue berry muffin, nice tradition.

I walked for kilometers in and out of shops looking and touching things, I must touch things, otherwise I don't buy it, I like to touch and liked to be touched, part of my life I never had, part that I missed out in life, to be touched.

What an enjoyable day in New York, no meetings, nothing to worry about, just me and New York.

I got off the plane and stand outside the airport to find a taxi cab, one of those yellow ones I hurt so many off, damn all of them are yellow and if I'm getting one where the hell must I go, what do I tell the cab driver where must he drop me.?

"Just don't panic," I keep on telling myself.

I opened the door of the first taxi I can reach, pushed my bag into the other side of the seat, the driver still wanted to put my bag in the boot,

"sorry, in America I keep my things close to me, went through my mind."

Where to sir?" the taxi driver asked. "New York please," I reply.

He looked at me with a smile on his face,

"I know New York sir, but where in New York?" he asked me with a twingle in his eyes.

I don't like this, to be in a corner in a country I don't know. I must think this through very quickly, his still looking at me, waiting for an answer.

"Can you take me to a place where I can sleep tonight that's not too expensive please?"

"I think I know exactly what you need sir, you need direction in New York, don't worry I will get you to a place you can afford."

"Thank you driver," and I feel much better already.

I'm only going to be in America for two months, and I worked my finances out onto the last dollar, if I do get some work on farms it can change my financial situation a little bit.

The taxi driver (John) were very kind, he dropped me at a very cheap overnight place to sleep, somebody he knows, after he spoke to the person, I got it for cheaper, I booked in for a week and saved thirty dollars.

John gave me his telephone number and made me promise that I will phone him if I get lost, or need a taxi to take me site seeing in New York.

I took a shower and smashed that bed with a deep sleep, tired after thousands of kilometers somewhere in the world. I woke up the next morning at about 9 am.

The owner must have hurt that I'm awake, he knocked on the door, as I opened the door he was standing there with one of the nicest smelling breakfast in his hands, I looked at the food and then at him.

"Morning it's on the house, he said," before I could say good morning.

"Uh, good morning and thank you,"

"it's nothing, it's good to have someone here from South Africa, never met a South African, just feel welcome here."

He left me with the food and closed the door behind him, what a nice meal, my first in America.

New York, New York, I'm in New York. I strolled down Broadway and can't believe what I'm seeing, buildings taller than, taller than what . . . , ? streets wider, wider than . . . , forget it; I'm going to enjoy this city for this coming week, and try to visit coffee shops as many as possible, must find a baycall and star bucks coffee, just to experience it, must put a photo in for you as reader of my first star bucks coffee.

There's something about this city that's just special, maybe these old steel bridges over to Manhattan river, or these old parking meters, or these old buildings with the stairs on the outside, dated out of the early days of New York, or maybe the old and new combination, whatever the case might be, I like New York. A lot of brain power went into this city, the creativity over all these years, and today it supply so many work and other business opportunities to look after families in America.

I forgot to phone my father in time, as I get back to the hotel he already left two messages at the receptionist; I must phone him as soon as I get to the hotel, the person at the reception counter made the call and allow me to speak to my dad as soon as he answers his phone. "Hallo dad . . . ." I promise to phone him every second day.

I went to my room and unpack some of my things for the week. Take a long shower and dry my long blond hair with their fixed blow dryer. Tomorrow I must pick up my car from the car rental I have booked before I left Texas. I like my hair in the wind and got a Porsche convertible, to do site seeing and it will be a pleasure to travel to Texas with it. Just me the Porsche and the wind, perfect . . . .

My third day in New York, today I'm going to travel north to Vermont just to see the country side away from the city 3-4 hours drive. I left early before the traffic gets too much, if I can push a little faster I can have breakfast in a diner somewhere in Vermont. I can feel the winter is getting closer, if I have problems with the convertible because of the cold temperatures, I will just change it for another one that can handle the chillness.

I called John the second day to find out if his available to take me for site seeing, "no problem sir, meet you at 8 am, thank you John." John arrived with his private vehicle, looks like a ship without a roof; it's his day of and decided to take me site seeing on his cost in and around New York.

My name in the American language will also be John, so off we go, the black John taxi driver and the white John hitch hiker combination.

What a perfect connection in America, John Black American X John White South African.

"John is it possible to stop at a pizza hut?"

"No problem Johnny."

We enjoyed all kinds of pizza and bottomless coke for lunch. It's good to have this man as a friend; he's the type that will walk the walk with his friends.

I have learned a lot about America (New York) from John Black (Johnson). The big lady is much bigger than in the movies, the streets much wider and vehicles much bigger, and the people are much faster than the people in South Africa. They think the way I want to think, "BIG". In South Africa there's a problem with people thinking "BIG" the other South African people don't understand you, or maybe they don't want to understand you.

John, this is one person I can contact every time I visit New York and will have no problem to get around this city. We travelled many miles that day and he insist that I have supper with his family that evening, he already phoned his wife earlier that day without me knowing it, when we got to his house, I met the nicest women and a absolute much for John, a women with a tender heart for a family, you can see this is a women that knows how to support her husband. "Tephany", no it can't be my favorite name, engraved into a waterfall step in South Africa. What does that mean, Tephany in America? I don't know, not yet.

I looked at the food on the table and then at the children and his wife, there's something about black people I don't understand, they can be poor, but let me tell you one thing; they can fill a table with food. They look after their families white people can only think of.

I had one of the best evenings of my life, and that in America, Tephany felt like a mother to me, I had another two suppers with them in that week.

The time with the black Johnsons took me back many years ago at the age of I think two years before I went to the orphanage, I lived with black people and remember the time we use to eat porridge, only porridge together, poor. They have taught me to take a small piece of porridge and then I must role a small ball between my two hand palms to cool it down before I can put it in my mouth to eat.

Tomorrow John will help me to get onto a Greyhound bus on my way to Texas, what a good black man, husband, father and friend, well balanced human being.

I like Vermont, it so peacefull; the people are in a slower gear in this part of the world, here they have time for each other, they think different, more human. When you sit at a diner for a meal it will be much more casual than in the city, it's nice, I like it to be treated like a normal person.

They are busy making ice from the river water for thanksgiving weekend; you can see ice cannons shooting snow on the mountain slopes, looks like the snow is a little late this year. (I like this idea of making snow) the area are coverd with a layer of snow, but it will not be thick enougth for skiing.

Thanksgiving, it's the first year that I will not be at home for this special weekend, a weekend to remind us about the past of America, to say thanks for where we came from. I personally think it is only for white people and for those who made peace to be here from other countries against their will. Wonder sometimes how the Indian people must feel about thanksgiving weekend? One thing about the past we can't cling to, people do make mistakes all over the wold, but it's our responsibility to make peace and help those we can reach today for a new future. We must learn out of the mistakes they made in the past and just better on it, must be part of our daily living.

I'm back in New York in my hotel room, two days before I leave for my trip back to Texas. I phoned my dad to let him know that I will phone him before I leave for Texas. He wants me to pick some documents up on the last morning before I leave New York.

"**My** last morning," I have packed my bag the night before to be ready for John to pick me up at 9 am.

I greeted the owner of the overnight guest house and put my 30 kilogram bag on my back, I connect all the clips and it feels solid on my back, I walked to the end of the pavement, (walkway) looked for traffic, see no traffic and starting to walk to the other side of the road where John is waiting for me.

I woke up in the hospital two days later, and don't know where I am. John his wife and the overnight room owner were standing next to my bed with sad faces.

"**My** last day, I overslept and wanted to pick my father's documents up at 8 am, it's already 9 am. I pushed the accelerator in a little more to make the green light, the next moment a hitch hiker stepped right in front of my Porsche, I hit him with the rigth front fender and he misses my head with inches as he role over the car and landed on the back of the Porsche and then onto the tar road, I stopped ten meters from the hiker, his not moving, his bag is lying on top of him".
"Damn"!!!No sign of life in him.

Everything came to a dead stop in the road, a taxi driver parked his taxi across the road to make sure he stop all the traffic, he got out of the yellow taxi and ran while calling a name,

"John, Johnny are you all right?" no responds, John is lying dead still, I ran back to the hiker with a shock

I can't handle, I fell in the tar road on my one knee, the blood is running down my leg but I don't feel any pain.

The ambulance was on the accident scene in seconds, people are all over the area. It's like a movie, everybody wants to get a chance to look. The medics had to cut his bag from his back before they could turn John around; I see blood running from his left eye down his cheek onto the tar road. After the medics done their inspection on his neck and back for injury, they found that he had broken ribs, concussion and bruses.

They load him very carefully on the stretcher and into the ambulance. The ambulance drove away on high speed to the hospital. I had to stay at the accident scene for an accident report. The Porsche is in a bad condition, right head light in pieces, dented and windscreen badly damage.

I phoned my dad, he kept quiet while listening to my story, his not answering after I have stopped talking, seconds went by, and I know his thinking . . . "I'm alright, don't worry."

"And the pedestrian" came his voice over the phone,

"I forgot all about the hiker, sorry dad I have to go, I phone you when I know more, bi."

The taxi driver gave me his card before he left with the hiker to the hospital; I found the card with his number on it in my jacket. I phoned the number and a woman answered the phone, she directed me to the hospital where the hiker is taken. I took a cab to the

hospital; there is still dry blood on my knee when I got to the hospital.

The taxi driver and another man is standing in the hallway, he came straight to me when he saw me.

"MY name is Tephany," and put my hand out to greet him.

"I'm John, please to meet you Tephany," said John,

"Do you know anything about the hiker John?" I asked.

John explains the whole story about the week they spend with the hiker.

"The doctor said we will be able to see him in an hour or so, you can wait if you want to, or maybe get some rest at the hotel, I will phone you later."

"no I wait with you,"

John asks the nurse to clean my knee while we are waiting for the doctor.

Concussion, cut under the left eye and three broken ribs and in a deep sleep.

According to his doctor he must rest for two days and stay in hospital for at least one week for observation. We were allowed to visit him for ten minutes. Three quarter of his face is been bandage, he lie peace full like a mummy, his arms on top of the blanket on the side of his body, his well formed fore arms and hands make a impression on me.

I went back to the hotel and booked myself in for another week, I fell onto the bed and cried like a little girl, I emptied the box of hotel tissues and used the toilet paper to wipe my tears and nose. I ordered some sugar water to get over the shock of the accident. Plans, what plans? I don't have any more plans for this holiday, I can't just leave this man from Africa here in a New York hospital, he need some support. It's the least I can do.

I don't feel like going out of my room for dinner, I placed an order for room service just to get some food in my body. I took a long shower and wish I can wash this whole day out of my system. I'm laying on top of my blankets with my peach colored gown on, I'm thinking about the accident, the well dressed hiker in front of me looking the other way as he stepped in front of my car, why would he look to the opposite direction when he wants to cross a busy road in New York? his body flying over my head hitting the back of the car before landing onto the tar road.

Now must I sit with this burden for the rest of my life. More tears are streaming from my eyes.

I looked at his face again there on the road after the medics turned him around, the blood running from the open wound under his left . . . . Something is not right, brown hair, cut under the left eye and, yes there was tears running down his cheeks as well, onto a black floor, the tar road are black. His face was calm because he was unconscious. It must be him, yes it must be!!

I jumped up and get dressed in seconds, I want to be next to his bed, I took a cab to the hospital and ask the driver to go faster, he just looked at me and know it must be an emergency.

I sit next to his bed and put my hand softly on his hand, it's warm and strong and I can see the Africa tan on his arm and hand, for the first time in twelve years I can touch my husband, what a good feeling, my hand is about two thirds of his. There is peace in my heart when I touch his hand, I longed for this moment for so many years.

Hallo John, my name is Tephany, please to meet you,"
"**I'm** sorry what happened to you today."

I couldn't stop the tears from running down my cheeks, I don't care, I want to cry and I don't even wipe the tears away.
"**I** nearly killed my husband without knowing that it's him,"
I just wept more, all these years nearly for nothing. The sister brought me a glass of hot milk and a blanket to cover my legs.

"**Maybe** you can hear me, I am from Texas and came to New York for a holiday, I prayed many years for you and didn't know we are going to meet under these circumstances,"

I cried again, I just can't control my tears, "but I'm happy, happy for us. Just want to say that you are a very special part of my life for the last twelve years, my birthday is coming up on the11[th] December and I hope you can be with me to celebrate it."
"It's his birthday too you know, maybe you can do something together."

As I turned around I look straight into the face of the sister,

"**Close** your mouth honey, its true," she just smiled and walk away.

I took his hospital file and open it to make sure the sister doesn't miss it, 11th December . . . . What more do I need to be sure? Nothing.

I feel so good and sad at the same time, sad that John can't feel the same as I do. The sister wakes me up early the next morning, "I think you must go and get a shower and clean clothes on you, don't worry he will still be here when you get back."

"Think it will do me good to feel better, thank you sister."

I don't know myself, something is been happening to me, something I don't know, l can't explain it, but it feels damn good. This is the day I was waiting for, for twelve years, the person, the one that must fill the vacuum in my heart, yes that must be the part that came to life. I'm just happy!!!

I had the best shower ever in my life, I have met "MY MAN." I dressed myself like never before; I comd my hair with a song in my heart and make sure it shines like the sun. Everything looks so new, and the people look so happy today.

When I got to the hospital, John and his wife waited for me at the entrance, I greet them with a handshake and we walked to John's room, its ten in the morning and visiting time for the patients. They removed the bandage from John's head earlier the morning, the left side of his face are badly swollen and blue from the cut under the eye or a knock somewhere on the vehicle or tar road.

John is still sleeping, I stayed there long after John and his wife left. I can't look enough at the man I've waited for so long.

"I love you John, for so many years I wanted to say it to you. I say it because I really mean it."

"I love you John", "I love you John,"

"I love you John," for the first time in my life the words are making sense, words I never used in my life before, I only hurt it from my mother. She said she loved me during the day and after she put me into bed at bedtime for my bedtime story.

I kissed him softly on the forehead before I left and it felt so good when my lips touches his skin, I wish I can kiss him on his lips, but that is one thing I will leave for him to do, he must make the first move to kiss me, and it will be good to wait for him.

When I got to the hotel the receptionist handed me the key for the new car the car rental company delivered earlier that morning. There's also a message that I must phone my dad. "My dad," what and how will I tell my dad about this man in my life? How do I explain a twelve year relationship with a man I never knew, to a Texas business man called my father, with a look nobody likes?

I'm twenty eigth and a succesfull business woman, and I think I have enough self convidence to discus the matter with him in the way he knows best, business wise. I will give him the facts on the table, where will I get the facts? I still have a month and a half to go; surely something will come up before we see each other face to face.

I can't move, there must be something wrong with me, I can't keep my eyes open, and this pain in my head is killing me, my chest,? what went wrong, "where am I?" I try to concentrate, but I'm too tired . . . ."

I woke up in the middle of the night with pain too much to handle, I struggle to breath, someone mentioned my name and I can feel pain in my arm . . . .

When I opened my eyes I could only see with one eye, I saw John, his wife and the overnight guest house owner standing next to my bed. John put his hand softly on my right arm.

"Good morning John," he said. "You've been in an accident, but you are all right, you have concussion, some broken ribs and a cut under your left eye, that's the reason for seeing only out of the one eye. You must stay in hospital for another five days, doctor orders, but don't worry, we will come and visit you daily."

I struggle to open my mouth to say something, it's too much swollen. I closed my eyes and never saw them leaving.

I had a dream about a "Angel" standing next to my bed saying something about love and sorry and Texas, I couldn't get the whole sentence, but her face were shining like the sun, her face totally covered by the brightness.

I felt the tender touch on my right hand, it's like cool water, just the right temperature to collapse my whole inside into a calmness I don't know of, touched by an

Angel, what a good feeling. When she left I could feel the loneliness coming into my heart, I wanted to call her back, but I can't get my mouth open, I can see only her long shiny hair as she walked away, she's gone, will I see her again?

I opened my eyes on the third day in hospital, its still dark, there's someone sitting in a chair in the dark, could be the Angel I saw yesterday, I recognize her on the blond hair, it looks so beautifull, I don't want to wake her up, it doesn't feel good when she leaves.

I'm going to take a change to take one big change but I'm sure it's the right thing to do. "Tephany", can you hear me? Her eyes flew open and she jumped out of the chair, "yes John?" She answered. The next moment she is standing right next to my bed. I looked her straight in the eyes, I see tears running down her cheeks, and she just stood there, her hand in mine. I feel the same calmness I felt yesterday when she touched my hand.

"Is your name Tephany?" "yes I'm Tephany," I knew it, I just knew it. I knew that I will meet my future wife in America.

"But what are you doing here in the hospital are you a sister," no, I'm part of the reason your in the hospital, I ran you over with my car," he just looked at me with no emotion on his face, suppose there must be a good explanation for that, he said. "**He** left it there.

"Where are you from?" he asked.
"Texas," I answered.

"I'm also on my way to Texas," he said."
"You can get a lift with me if you like,"
"with you, are you sure it will be safe?"
I can see the twingle in his eye,
"just for the record, you walked in front of my car, I didn't hit you on the side way."

John and his wife visited us at 9: am. and brought some snacks to eat. I struggle to get food in my body because of my swollen face, but the staff has many patience. They know I must eat to stay strong.

It's a suffering to lie in this hospital; I must make a plan to get out of this bed. There is a window on the other side of the room. After John and them left I put my legs down from the bed and can feel the pain in my chest, I pushed myself onto my feet and walked slowly towards the window and reach it with lots of pain,
"sorry pain, I can't lay down for another day."

I looked over the city and enjoy the view. The big sister gives a whistle when she came in. "I knew you were one of those that can't stay in bed," and left me to do my own thing.

I walked to the toilet, and then visit some of the patients in my ward on my way back to my bed, as I turn around from the last patient to go back to my bed, I saw the most beautiful women standing next to my bed, her blue eyes looking through me and straight into my heart. She wanted to support me, but I stopped her with a hand wave, as I got to my bed she helped me onto the bed and it feels good to lie down.

"**Hallo** Tephany," "hallo John are you ready to go home," "If you will take care of me?"

There is something between us I can't explain, something so strong and special we bove can feel in this world that we still don't understand.

"**I'm** waiting for the doctor to sign me out, maybe today."

"Why are you still visiting me Tephany?"

The question nearly knocks me over. I looked at him with something in my heart for this man that grew so strong over the last twelve years and it forched me to tell him the truth about him as my husband for the last twelve years.

"**John,** I made a disition twelve years ago on my sixteenth birthday next to a river to build a relationship with my future husband, and got dreams about you over the years, the brown hair, cut under the left eye, blood and tears running down your cheeks onto a black floor, the tar road, when I saw you lying on the tar road of New York, peace were shining from your face even with your eyes closed, peace only I could see of all the people that were standing around you that day. I never thought I would be the one to run you over in a city called New York we both love so much."

"**So** the truth is, you are already my husband for tvelve years and my heart ached for you for so many years, I just wanted to be with you, but I never knew that you will be someone from a country called "South Africa." It's not from where you are but who you are."

I looked at her and the tears are running down my cheeks, tears of joy, tears of love, love for this women I longed for so many years to fill a gap in my heart to cover all the pain and fix all the scars life has given me. Is it possible that two people from different countries can live so long with decire for each other and meet in a place like New York, New York the "Unity City" for J and T, a beginning we will never forget. I will always carry the scars to prove it.

When she ended her story about me, I told her about the special way she came to me while traveling in my own country South Africa.

I looked for a women called; Tephany after I got her name on one of the steps at the most beautiful waterfall in South Africa called the "Mac Mac falls" in the eastern side of my country, somebody ingraved the name into a step. From that day on I travelled the whole country looking for this special woman to fill a gap in my life a man can't fill. "Tephany" a name you don't get very often in a country.

I went through hail, rain, wind, days, nights and the African sun to meet her here in the apple city, and in a hospital of all places, not a coffee shop, a hospital. But its fine with me, I met her and that is what counts. I learned to make peace over situations in my life very quickly, think about it sort it out, get an answer and carry on. Life is sometimes your enemy if you don't sort things out in your personal life, it will follow you where ever you go.

"So, our situation in New York is like a feary tale that we can tell to many around the table in the future."

The doctor alowed me to leave the hospital on the fifth day, what relieve. Tephany booked me in the same hotel she is staying in; she spoke to the hotel manager and got the room next to hers to look after me for he next week. As I get to my room she opened the door for me to go in, on my bed stands a new back pack, mine was ripped open in the accident and twelve most beuatifull roses on the huge pillows on my bed, the twelve years she waited for me. A yellow light weight wheel chair is standing next to my bed for her to push me where ever we want to go.

This women can think, not just think she can do thinks as well, I like that in a person, if you say something you must do it, otherwise you will have no balance in your personal life.

I gave her a soft hug to thank her, she laid her head on my chest for two seconds, a feeling I never forgot. She order room sevice and we had our first dinner around a table she especially ordered for this first evening. alone on the balcony with the most beautifull view over New York City, and a outstanding women with a feeling I need more of in my life.

We just enjoyed each others closeness and I was telling her about the bush and the hunting and my hitch hiking to motivate people to carry on in life.

Every time our eyes make contact we can feel the urge to be closer to each other, there is something around us that I hope will stay around us forever, a type of love that's there for many years already, but tonight we can feel it much stronger than ever before, because we are together and that makes it much more special. It's a unity that we can't descripe; you must feel it yourself to understand it.

She made sure that I'm in bed at nine and I don't kick against her discipline. I looked at her while she's working towards the door, but she stopped before she opens the door, turns around and put her soft lips on my forehead, "I love you John" and left me wide awake for another hour before I fel into a peacefull sleep.

She woke me up with a gentle hand over my fore head; I looked at her in the halfdark room.
"John it's medicine time,"
"what time is it?"
"12:15 am." she answerd. She woke me again at 04.00 am.

When she came into my room at seven, I was standing in the shower, my first shower in seven days. I looked at all the bruses on my body, that Porsche got hold of me. John the taxi driver explained the whole accident to us earlier, before I start to cross the road I looked in the wrong direction, the way Tephany saw it as well, it struck me, I'm use to look in that direction in South Africa, because we are driving on the left side of the road, and it's so easy to make a mistake in a country where they drive on the right hand side of the road. Tephany felt much better after we have sorted this mistery out.

I opened the shower door and hear soft music in the room, the nurse is here already, I get the smell of coffee and bacon hanging in the air," I'm hungery."

I struggled to get my hotel gown on. I got out of the bathroom and saw her sitting on the sofa waiting for me; I see a lot of patients in her. She got up when she sees me; I walk like an old man. "Good morning to my patient and how do you feel this morning?" "good morning nurse, sore but better than yesterday morning, thanks to you." She fixed the table for breakfast and pulled the chair out so that I can get onto it. "Thanks Tephany," "pleasure John." My medicine is standing on the table next to a glass of water, for after breakfast. This girl is thinking ahead, I like it; she likes to do some planning.

After breakfast and medicine I got dressed in my track suite to make it easy for the pain, I got into the wheel chair that looks like a marathon chair. Tephany is dressed in a white track suite with soft purple spots on the shoulders. She's got some hairy thing on her head. We are coverd for the streets of New York. She doesn't want to tell me what she has plan for the day. We walked straight to central park, I haven't seen nature for weeks, it's good to feel the cool temperature on my face, and I like this kind of weather.

"Can we have a garden like this one one day?" I asked. "everything is possible," She reply. I feel her tender hand on my shoulder; she is some one that needs closeness, I can't count how many times she touched me today, just to tell me she's here for me. I never knew a person like this before and never in my life somebody touching me with so much gentleness in my whole life.

She doesn't know it, but she is filling a gap in my heart that I longed for so many years on this earth, to be touched, day and night. She is special and we are very happy, it feels like many years that we are together already. We looked at each other.

She stopped at a green patch of gras, she helped me out of the wheel chair and we sat there looking at the people passing us by. Young people, old couples and children playing on the gras with no fear.

We have visited the nicest coffee shops on her planned mission, we enjoyed bayculs and blueberry muffins not without starbucks coffee of cause. She showed me the coca cola shop, everything with the coca cola color and badge on it; she bought two coca cola hats.

She pushed me most of the day from shop to coffee shop, she is fit this girl and I like it. She doesn't forget, every four hours she will take the medicine and water out of the wheel chair bag and help me to get it in my body. The pain killer helps for the pain in my chest.

We arrived back at three in the afternoon at the hotel, I'm tired. She pushed the wheel chair next to the bed to make it easier for me to get onto my bed, as I lay down I could feel I need this rest. She coverd me with an extra blanket and I thanked her for the days outing. She looked at me with those special blue eyes, eyes with happiness in it, she kissed me on my fore head again, a place she claimed for herself to put her soft lips on and I like it, it lets me feel so good inside. "I enjoyed it to; it's good to be with you."

I closed my eyes and fel a sleep emediatly.

She woke me up at six that evening, and asked me to get ready; she booked a table for us in the hotel.

I took a shower and when I got out she has put my clothes nicely on the bed, she made my bed, wow!! I got dressed, she left a note that she will see me at 19.15 pm.

There is a knock on the door and when she opened the door I'm already in the wheel chair with a smile on my face,
"come, come the food is getting cold," I joked.
She laughed for the first time so loud of happiness that she had to put her hand on her mouth to stop herself from laughing to loud.

She pushes me to an area that's leading to the top of the hotel,
"where are we going," I asked.
She just put her her finger in front of her mouth with a "shh," sound.

Another secret plan I believe. Someone opened the door onto the hotel roof, and she pushes me to a big table with a lot of people around it, as we get closer I recognise John the black taxi driver, his wife and all their children, the guest house owner and his wife, the sister from the hospital. She even got hold of the ambulance staff that helped me with the accident. The hotel manager were sitting on my left hand side and Tephany on my other side, with her hand as usual softly on my hand I can do business with this women, she likes to give back to people, what a special gift, givers will always be rich people, not always in the financial side, but in their inner being.

We enjoyed the evening with laughter till late. She has the ability to do things that anybody will remember for the rest of their lifes.

We left earlier than the other guests; she pushes me back after we have greeted everybody. I feel like a man with happiness I can't describe to myself, it's just growing everyday with speed I like.

She opened my door, as she turn around to push me into my room I stand up out of the chair and kissed her softly on her cheek as I pull her closer towards me, she put her arms around my middle and we stand like that for a while.

I looked down at her and see the tears running down her cheeks again, and I know it's about happiness. "I love you Tephany, and will always do." I wish to kiss her on her mouth, but my mouth is still swollen, and she knows that to. I will wait for a special moment, and know we will enjoy it.

Our last day in New York, we did some route planning after we had breakfast together, it feels good to do something with some one, we discus the the orpenhage vouchers and brought in a maintenance plan to keep the buildings in good shape through the year.

The more I get to know John, the more I get the idea of a business partner for the future, his ideas are much different than the American people and it's maybe a good idea to combine these African ideas with the American way. I never thought of maintenance on orphanage buildings, if you better the child living and playing area you will have a much more positive child in the future. You must always have a plan before you give finances to aid.

We can help in the beginning to get everything up to standard, and then start businesses and use the profit for the orphanages, it will create work and will be tax free, so that means more money to help children in need.

Give and forget doesn't work. Give with a well structured plan will always work, it force some discipline onto the people that's running the orphanage. We don't give money, we pay what they need and then get it deliverd at the orphanage.

I pushed John to central park after lunch. We sat on one of the benches and drink nature in with our eyes.

"What happened to your mother?" came the question like an apache arrow straight through my heart, I truggle to breath, I feel sick. John sees that I'm uncomfortable and felt terrible. He put his arm around me with tenderness. "Sorry,"

This man is my husband; I must tell him about my mother, I haven't spoken about her in twenty years. I believe this man is here to help me with things of my past that's holding me back from a special future, he just asked the right questions very straight and not all of them are nice but it can make me free if I talk about it. He is the right person to dicuss it with.

"I had the most beautifull mother on this planet; she was born with a song in her heart. She use to sing songs to me from the day she discovered she was pregnant with me, any kind of positive songs."

"She waited for me with a heart full of joy, she will walk in the field and tell me all about nature, birds, insects and any thing she can find on our farm she would think will make me a better person. She went through story books like a printer.

After I got born she picked up the pace of learning me on the natural way even more, she learned me the practicle side of life that matters the most, how to stay alive with the circumstances your in, to feel for people you don't even know, nobody asked to be on this planet." John is playng with my hair while I'm taking my thoughts back to those years that matters so much to me.

It feels good to get this burden of my heart with someone I can trust. John's a good listener. He will ask one question and will then listen to the whole answer before saying anything. That's part of my dad I also admire, he will never cut in while you busy talking. If you cut into a conversation you can loose good knowledge, he once said.

My mother could play the quitar with passion, she will sit in my room and just let her fingers run over the strings till I close my eyes for a good night rest.

Where ever my mother went she will take me with, she had a white (her fouverite color) two seater covertable, we enjoyed it when the wind blows through our hair.

One day my mother had a apointment in town, she dressed me like a princes, as we got out the house my father ask if I don't rather want to go with him today, his going to fly over the farms to do inspection like his doing often. I look at my mom and she could see that I want to go flying with my dad.

"Its fine with me if you want to go flying honey," she said.

She gave me a kiss on my fore head and left for town in her convertable.

My father picked me up and put me on his one shoulder, he walked to the barn with me to start the plane. We flew along the river and as we turn to follow the tar road an emergency call came over the radio in the cockpit, asking that my dad must come in imidiatly.

There has been an accident. "what kind of accident is it daddy," I wanted to know from him. "I don't know Angel, we will hear after we have landed." I could see my father is worried.

There is a sherrifs vehicle and some other vehicles that been waiting for us as we approache the landing strip that ran on the side of the barn. When we got out of the plane the sherrif came to my dad and took him one side, a sherrif woman took me one side and asks me questions about the flight we just had. I looked back to where my father is standing and could see how his moving his head from side to side while his looking down towards the ground.

The sherrif women start to ask me questions about killer bees.

"Do you know killer bees Angel," "nope" came my answer,

"only bees my mammy told me about."

Your mommy had an accident today after bees attacked her on her way to town."

"Is she dead" I imidiatly ask the women, "yes Angel, I'm sorry," I start to cry very softly and the women held me against her for a while.

My dad took me from the women and we cried together. He saved my life that day by asking me to go flying with him.

I'm still missing my mom today, and I know my dad to. He never married again and looked after me till I could look after myself. He barried her on our farm, the farm he gave to me when I turned sixteen.

We have visited her grave many times over the last twenty four years and every year on her birthday we will put fresh roses on her grave. My mother died on the age of twenty eigth, I was four years and six months old. My father was thirty two years in the year of the accident.

"So my hitch hiking friend with the broken ribs, this is my mother's story and I'm feeling much better after twenty four years, I could never speak to my father about it, he is still walking around without peace in his heart since the day of the accident. Maybe you will be able to help him as a friend to get him to the point of peace making, who knows" it will be a good thing to get my father back I have lost twenty four years ago."

"You are straight enough to handle him, and he will admire you for that, you both have answers for other peoples problems, the only difference is that you made peace about your past and know how to help people with passion, passion he doesn't have, not yet"

"You are rite about the fact that I made peace about my past, but there will always be this piece about a father in this case that's missing forever, a father to discuss things with, play with in a garden, fishing with, get hugged by, just to do things with. A dad that can call you, send you somewhere, a dads voice that's been part of your life as a child. Someone you can go to when you're scared, to take you in his arms where you can feel save. Every child needs a father as a role model. A dads voice you can remember forever in your memory after he left this world."

"**I** can't handle it anymore, it's getting too much for me, my tears are running like a river while his telling me about the part of a father that's missing in his life, I never thought of all these things about a dads role that is so important in a childs life, and this man missed out on all of that. I wish I can fill the gap in his heart, but I know peace did it already, I feel thankfull for the word peace. It can set so many people free."

I love my dad with a new kind of love, I'm going to tell him that I'm sorry about my mother and that I love him with a special love just for him, a daugthers love, that will be my first words when I see him again.

I will start all over again with our relationship, our children needs a grandfather with feelings, feelings without business, a real grandfather that can sit next to the river with them, learn them how to catch a fish. They need a grandfather without all the travelling in his life, a relaxed man every day of his life.

We will handle the businesses and look after him for the rest of his life that's left. I will show John everything about the business; his got a strong personality and enough discipline to handle the staff.

I found a real African diamond in New York. He looked at me and wiped the tears away with his hanky." Don't worry Angel, we will make it, and we're going to make it big," he said as he looked into my eyes, I feel the peace running through me when I looked into that green eyes with only one message to my heart, "peace."

The only reason I believe in this relationship is because it started so many years ago for us.

We are not in a hurry when we woke up the next morning; it feels good to stand under the water in the shower with no need to be some where. We have decided to leave New York at eleven in the morning and will drive till seven and book into any overnight place a hitch hiker can't afford, Tephany's idea, she insist to tread me all the way back to Texas, "only if I can organize our birthdays" I said. "Okay" and looked me in my eyes with a smile and pushed her head against my chest. This woman knows I like to be touched.

We booked out of the hotel with good friends greeting us, friends that will never forget us, because of the accident hitch hiker, and it will be memories that will stay there for a very long time. Why? We bought that hotel later in our lifes to send people there to relax, part of giving back to people. I let them framed that old cut to pieces back pack of mine and put him in the lounge area with the whole story, to motivate people to carry on with their dreams, because dreams are there to keep us alive.

We made John Johnson the taxi driver a partner in the hotel, and he and his whole family moved to a house we invested in them on his birthday, If a person wants to do something for another person, why not helping him.

We build a clinic for children on the third floor and the sister that helped me with so many patience got the opportunity to help many children over the years in New York City, a clinic with his own bus service and mobile clinics to get to people as far as Vermont. Prevention is better than cure. You help children early in their lives; you will have great leaders for the future in their own city and country.

We got into the Porche and took of; just outside New York she stopped, we got out of the car and looked back towards the city that brought us together in a way. I pulled her close to me and stand there with no words, just a picture in front of us, **New York City**.

It's good to be with someone that knows her country like Tephany. She knows how to handle them on a business level where ever we stop, I learned a lot from her on our way to Texas. She's in another laugue, whether they know her or not, they respect her for her way.

We have done several orphanages on our way already and she cried her into another world every time we leave those children and staff behind. I bougth a couple boxes of tissues after the first orphanage we visited.

Tomorrow wil be our birthdays, and I'm still planning the coffee shop idea, I think I can affort it. I saved a lot of money for not paying for much on the road; Tephany used her card and putting the payments through the business.

Sorry, but tomorrow will be on me, and she knows it. We gatherd all the info we needed to put the orphanages onto our giving list.

We thought of a business we can start when we get to the end of our holiday, we want to get Texan women involved to help with this orphanage idea country wide, why doing it on our own, more people less work, this man enreach my heart with his passionate ideas for helping other people. His not just a giver, no plan no giving, strictly business.

We found this nice hotel to stay in, plane but nice, friendly people. I looked at the women with the big smile behind the reception desk, this must be my contact, she's friendly enough and she will be able to help me getting this birthday idea of the floor. We decided to call a early early evening, we were busy the last couple of days, and I can see Tephany's in a tired bracket, as soon as I'm in my room I phoned the women down stares to know if I can come and see her, "yes sir" she answerd.

As we drove in earlier I saw this coffee shop next to the hotel, it happens to be the same owner as the hotel. I booked the whole coffee shop after I got a price for a baycoll and coffee for twenty people.

I asked the hotel women to invite twenty guests for a free baycoll and coffee at seven sharp, and if they can sing Amazing grace when the women with the blond hair comes through the door. Everything set for a nice coffee shop birthday. I got twenty eigth roses after hours from someone the hotel lady new.

I woke Tephany up early the next mornig, to get ready for the road, I packed our luagage in the car and take her gentle on her arm and steer her towards the coffee shop, and everybody is waiting for the big moment. As she walks through the door a woman starts to sing with the most beautifull voice I have ever heart, "Amazing grace how greate thow are . . . ," and a elderly women handed her the twenty eight red roses. Tephany looked at me and I give her one of my best smiles, everybody follow the women softly in song. The tears are running again, I hold her and wish I can hold her for ever.

We decided to stay for another day, another hotel we bougth later in our lifes to add onto our "giving something back to people, also with a clinic, everything paid for." If there is something wrong with a child we as adults must do something to help. A child doesn't want to know about money, or there is no food or clothes, they just want to play. They don't make sums to see if there is money to help themselves; it's our responsibility to make sure there is enough to look after them.

We are going through areas that are so amazing for the eye to see. It feels so good to be part of this world. I am thinking of this new world I'm going to stay in for the rest of my life. A world people will understand the way I'm think. If I think "BIG" I will be able to do big things as well. With a wife like Tephany I will surely have the backing to do great things, not just for other people but also for our own children, to create a way of living that will make them new leaders for a new generation, a caring generation. We need balance in life, "talk and do."

We are nearly on the end of our journey; we became the best friends on this planet, I looked at John with my heart and can feel how we connect every time we are looking or touching each other, I know he want's to kiss me, I feel it strong in my heart and I sometimes feel like walking up to him and take it from his lips, but I made a promise to myself that he must make that move first. I know his waiting for the rite moment and that it must be special for both of us, something to remember for the rest of our future.

In my whole life not one man has kissed me, that's why this kiss will be like something that will rock my brain, another new experience I'm looking forward to enjoy. (Twenty eight and never been kissed) I know I will make it up with this man. I kept it for so long inside me for the rite person, and know I will give it all at the rite time, and I have met the person Im going to give it to, John the man I longed for twelve years, the man with the African tan that pulls me like a magnet every time

I see him or think about him. We are made for each other. I like to strole my hand over his arm, it's If the hair on his arm just makes me feel more like a women, and he will look at me with eyes and a smile that awakes my whole inside, it's a pleasure to brake through this borders I don't know about.

We both can feel that we are building up to a point we will not be able to handle it anymore to stay away from each other, but we work hard on it not to go to far, there is still a whole future lying ahead of us.

I like the way we have started, (not the accident) as friends, friends for life and then a couple that will grow stronger as we go on in our new future together.

I phoned my dad four days ago to tell him that I'm bringing an extra worker that's going to help us on the farm. He just kept quiet again as usual when he thinks. "Lets see want comes up Angel," he said.

As we drove onto the farm, I saw my father come out the front door, he build one of those big city houses on the farm, as you already know, not my stile, as long as his happy, I'm happy.

We got out the Porche and I put my arms around him and give him a kiss on both his cheeks, "hallo dad," he looked at me with a big questionmark on his face, he struggle to handle my freedom. He is happy to see me and walked over to John to take his hand, and welcome him on the farm.

I look her father in the eyes and we measure each other in seconds, his a head shorter than I am with a white mistarge and blond hair, not to much left in the front. "please to meet you Mr. Parker"

Her father invited us in and we enjoyed supper together. His a person with good qualities, I'm not a person that likes to talk to much in the beginning, must know the person a day or two before starting a conversation. Luckily his not the type of person that will force you into a conversation and I feel at ease with that.

I can see Tephany is in meetings with her dad for the next couple of days, not about us, but about their businesses. I'm staying in the town house about twenty meters from the main house. The garden is in a top condition, I like gardens, and this ones good on the eye.

On the third day I couldn't hold it back anymore, I took one of the horses and ride to see the cattle she was telling me about. I got back just before dinner and she is waiting for me at the stables.

"Hi, didn't know you can ride a horse mr. hitch hiker?" "there's still a lot of things you still have to learn about me blondè."

I took a shower and walked over the main house to have supper with Tephany, her father is out for two days and will arrive back the next day. As I entered the front door she came up to me and give me a hug, the first one in three days, we felt like two people become one without having sex, we stood like that for a while. We sat on the outside after dinner and discuss our future.

"Can we go to the river tomorrow," he asked.

"Yes, I want to show you something special at the river, we can leave just after breakfast"

He gave me one of those looks that pushes my whole inside overboard, I can't wait for our first night together, we will not sleep for that whole night. That's a promise, we will catch up for a whole week in a place nobody will know about.

As he walked away, I looked at him and can't resist it to run to him, I grap him on his arm to stop him, "John I just want to say I love you with my whole being."

He took my face into his two hands and kisses me softly on the forehead.

"**It** feels so good to be so close together."

"**I** love you to my Tephany from Texas."

We drove with the pick nick to the riverside. Tephany packed a pick nic basket for us to have lunch next to the river. As we got close to the river I saw the most beautifull tree house next to the river.

"**Who** build this house here on the river bank?"

"it's our house, I let it build especialy for us a couple of years ago."

"Do you like it."

"Do I like it? I love it, thatch roof and all"

We got out the vehicle and she opens the lift door for us to go in.

"Good idea with the winch Angel, you did everything so nice."

"I did it for us John, so that we can escape on weekends to a place nobody is allowed to come, only us as a family."

"**How** is it possible that I'm so lucky to have you in my life?" She just gave me a humble smile.

She stands with her back to me and I bend down and kiss her in her neck, she turns around and our lips make contact for the fist time in two months, she just let go, we kissed each other with passion and don't think of stopping, she pushes her body towards mine and I know we are not going to stop if I don't force us away from each other. I looked down into her soft blue eyes, and I ask something she's been waiting for twelve long years.

"Tephany?"

"yes John?" she looked at me with her soft blue eyes her mother build into her with tenderness.

"Will you marry me?"

The tears are running down her cheeks with the river running outside the tree house. I named that peace of river outside the treehouse, "**happy teardrop river**"

"Yes John, yes, I will marry you forever," came her answer, and I kissed her again just to say thankyou for a beginning of a future we have waited for so long.

"Can we sleep in the tree house for our first night after the wedding Tephany?" he asked with his lips close to my ear.

"Think it's a good idea John, the hotel will be to far anyway," I wispher while pulling him closer to me. I need more of this man; my heart can't get enough of him.

We stood on the balcony looking at the river with a glass of sjampain for the beginning of another new family here in "TEXAS"

Follow up;

The Hitch Hitch/Texas family

CHAPTER 1

BIBLIOGRAPHY

CURRICULUM VITAE